PENGUIN BOOKS
SELECTED POEMS

Kaifi Azmi is the most-awarded Urdu poet in the country. Awards he has won include the Padma Shri, the Sahitya Akademi Award, Afro-Asian Writers Lotus Award and the Maharashtra Gaurav Award. He has also been honoured with a doctorate from Vishva Bharati University, Shantiniketan. Kaifi Azmi is also the All India President of the Indian Peoples Theatre Association (IPTA). He is married to noted stage actress Shaukat Kaifi and has two children, Shabana and Baba Azmi.

*

Pavan K. Varma is a member of the Indian Foreign Service and has been posted in Bulgaria, Russia and at the Indian Mission to the United Nations in New York. He has been Press Secretary to the President of India; Joint Secretary, Africa, in the Ministry of External Affairs; and is currently Ambassador of India to Cyprus.

Besides the best-selling *The Great Indian Middle Class*, he is the author of *Ghalib: The Man, The Times*; *Krishna: The Playful Divine*; and *The Book of Krishna*. He also wrote *Maximize Your Life: An Action Plan for the Indian Middle Class* with Renuka Khandekar.

CU00683873

Selected Poems

Kaifi Azmi

Translated by Pavan K. Varma

PENGUIN BOOKS

An imprint of Penguin Random House

PENGUIN BOOKS

USA | Canada | UK | Ireland | Australia
New Zealand | India | South Africa | China

Penguin Books is part of the Penguin Random House group of companies
whose addresses can be found at global.penguinrandomhouse.com

Published by Penguin Random House India Pvt. Ltd
4th Floor, Capital Tower 1, MG Road,
Gurugram 122 002, Haryana, India

Penguin
Random House
India

First published in Viking by Penguin Books India 2001
Published in Penguin Books 2002

Copyright © Kaifi Azmi 2001
This translation copyright © Pavan Varma 2001

All rights reserved

15 14 13 12 11 10 9 8

ISBN 9780141004839

Typeset by Goel Colour Scan, New Delhi

Printed at Manipal Technologies Limited, India

This book is sold subject to the condition that it shall not, by way of trade
or otherwise, be lent, resold, hired out, or otherwise circulated without the
publisher's prior consent in any form of binding or cover other than that in
which it is published and without a similar condition including this condition
being imposed on the subsequent purchaser.

www.penguin.co.in

MIX
Paper from
responsible sources
FSC® C043100

अपनी बेटी शबाना के नाम
(For my daughter Shabana)

Selected Poems

क्रमांक

Contents

दो शब्द

मेरे दिल में बहुत दिनों से तम्मना थी कि मेरी नज़्मों का अंग्रेज़ी में कोई अच्छा तर्जुमा हो जाए। शुरू में मेरे दोस्त प्रितीश नन्दी ने कोशिश की और कुछ नज़्मों का तर्जुमा करके एक मुख़्तसर से किताब में शाया किया। उसके बाद भी कुछ दोस्तों ने कोशिश की लेकिन कामयाबी नहीं हुई।

मेरी बेटी शबाना आज़मी ने यह काम अपने जिम्मे ले लिया और एक क़ाबिल और सुख़नफहम मुतरजिम से कुछ नज़्मों का तर्जुमा कराया जिनसे मेरी कोई वाक़िफ़ियत नहीं थी हालाकि उनके काम और तर्जुमों से मैं बहुत मुतासिर था ख़ास तौर पे उस काम से जो उन्होंने ग़ालिब पर किया है।

जब मुझे पहली मर्तबा शबाना ने ये ख़बर सुनाई कि पवन वर्मा आपकी नज़्मों का तर्जुमा करेंगे और वो ही उसको किताबी शक्ल में छपवाएंगे भी तो मुझे लगा कि शबाना मुझे खुश करने के लिए ऐसा कह रही है लेकिन आज आपके और मेरे हाथ में जो किताब है वो मेरे ख़्वाब की ताबीर है इसलिए ये किताब अपनी बेटी शबाना आज़मी के नाम मानवन करता हूँ।

कैफ़ी आज़मी
दिसम्बर 2000

Author's Note

For a long time, I have nurtured the desire to see a good translation of my poems in English. Pritish Nandy, my good friend, had made an attempt and translated a few poems which were published in a slim volume. Later, a few other friends made the attempt without much success.

My daughter Shabana Azmi took it upon herself to accomplish the task and finally found a translator with a fine ear and a finer pen. I had not met him then but I was familiar with his work including his translations. In particular, I was well-acquainted with his work on Ghalib.

When Shabana first gave me the news that Pavan Varma would be translating my poems and would have them published, I thought Shabana was saying this only to please me. But, today, this book which is in my hands and in yours, symbolizes the fulfilment of my dreams, and for this reason I dedicate this book to Shabana Azmi.

Kaifi Azmi
December 2000

Translator's Note

Kaifi Azmi was born in 1918 in Azamgarh, UP. His nom-de-plume 'Azmi' is derived from his place of birth. His real name is Syed Athar Hussain Rizvi. Kaifi Saheb had his early education in Arabic and Persian in a traditional madrasa in Azamgarh. His first collection of poems entitled *Jhankar* was published in 1943. A second collection was published in 1947 with the title *Akhir-e-Shab*. *Awara Sajde*, his third collection, was published in 1973. This last work incorporating some of the poems of the earlier publications, won him the Sahitya Akademi Award. *Awara Sajde* was translated into Hindi in 1980. Since then several editions have been published. The poems in this translation have been selected primarily from *Awara Sajde*.

There are two prominent themes in Kaifi Azmi's poetry. One is love. The second deals with human struggle and, in particular, the plight of the poor and deprived. As a translator, I have never ceased to be amazed at the juxtaposition of both these themes in Kaifi Azmi's poems. Very early in his life Kaifi became a member of the Progressive Writers' movement. He is also a member of the Communist Party of India. For him, the cause of the exploited masses is not only a theoretical paradigm, but an emotional identification with the suffering of the dispossessed. It is for this reason that Kaifi is not content to be an armchair theoretician, remotely expounding the dialectical intricacies of social change. Kaifi is a spokesman of several workers' unions. He has carried his conviction to the battleground often participating in strikes and *dharnas*.

Kaifi Azmi, the romantic poet, appears almost incongruent when juxtaposed to the proletarian ardour of Comrade Azmi, the spokesman of the downtrodden. But the supposed distance between these two just does not exist for Kaifi. Kaifi refuses to be stereotyped. He is unwilling to yield the space of the romantic to the cause of the revolutionary. According to him, both coexist and revel in the sheer joy of living. The remarkable thing is that, to my mind, he is able to do justice to both these personas. His poetry effortlessly subsumes both these themes. He is passionate as the poet of love, and he is passionate as the poet of revolution. He is in love with life in all its vibrancy and plenitude. And I think, the reason he is able to be both the lover and revolutionary, without compromising either, is because he genuinely believes in the raison d'etre of both.

In any case, for all his involvement with the Communist Party, Kaifi Azmi can best be described as a man of conviction who refuses to be an ideologue. He has sought the unity of the like-minded, but chafed against the straitjacketing of the mind. He is sensitive to injustice, but impatient with any hamhanded attempts at intellectual regimentation. His intensity for certain causes has never succeeded in making him unidimensional. In fact, several of Kaifi's poems reflect his disillusionment at the failure of the radical left to live up to its own ideals. And, there is little doubt that the split within the Communist Party affected Kaifi in a far more personal way than it would have a traditional party apparatchik.

The seduction of Kaifi Azmi's poetry lies in its passion and its simplicity. Kaifi is a lover first, a poet later. He is a human being first, a writer later. Thus, there cannot but be a directness and spontaneity in the language and idiom of his poetry. He has never sought to be a poet confined to the literary elite. It is for this reason that he is exceptionally blunt in his resolute opposition to communalism—for it is a monstrosity that affects the common man the most.

Kaifi has successfully written for films too, and who can ever forget his immensely popular lyrics in films such as *Kaagaz ke Phool*. Some of his lyrics for Hindi films have also been translated in this selection. In fact, a great deal of Kaifi's work reflects his long sojourn in Bombay, where he could see at first-hand the searing divide between the rich and poor in India's commercial capital, witness the glitter of the film world and its often transparent artificiality, experience the occasional alienation generated by the impersonal hugeness of a metropolis, and feel a recurring nostalgia for his roots in his own village in Azamgarh.

I have greatly enjoyed translating these poems. For me, they have been both a revelation and, if I may confess, a relaxation. I enjoy translating poetry, a discovery I made first when I wrote my biography of Mirza Ghalib. *Awara Sajde* has travelled around the world with me. I have translated its *nazms* at airports, on flights, in trains, at home, on my farm, in Kasauli and elsewhere, and derived great pleasure in doing so. I have attempted to mostly translate in rhyme and metre, except when the original itself was in blank verse. This has imposed its own rigour and discipline and I have tried not to compromise in any way on the meaning and content of the poem. Only very rarely have the imperatives of rhyme and metre, prodded me into very marginally amending the literal meaning or sequence of a couplet or two. I am aware, of course, that all translations of great poetry cannot but be inadequate. If there are any shortcomings in the work, they are, without question, attributable to the translation.

The purpose of this labour would be served if Kaifi Azmi's work is introduced to a wider readership. There is a need to break the insular barriers created by language in our country. We must persevere in our attempt to introduce the largest number of people to the great reservoir of wisdom and understanding in the writings of people like Kaifi Saheb, who, at eighty-one, has literally been witness to an entire era, and whose dreams and aspirations for a great India have both fructified and remained unfulfilled.

At the end, I wish to put on record my gratitude to Shabana Azmi, whose enthusiasm in this project almost equalled mine. My gratitude is also due to my colleague, Mr Rohit Babbar, who painstakingly typed the manuscript. As always, I doff my hat to David Davidar, the CEO of Penguin India, and to his colleagues Ravi Singh and Aradhana Bisht, who helped put the book together.

Pavan K. Varma
December 2000

मकान

आज की रात बहुत गर्म हवा चलती है
आज की रात न फ़ुटपाथ पे नींद आयेगी
सब उठो, मैं भी उठूँ, तुम भी उठो, तुम भी उठो
कोई खिड़की इसी दीवार में खुल जायेगी

ये ज़मीं तब भी निगल लेने पे आमादा थी
पाँव जब टूटती शाख़ों से उतारे हमने
इन मकानों को ख़बर है न मकीनों[1] को ख़बर
उन दिनों की जो गुफाओं में गुज़ारे हमने

हाथ ढलते गये साँचे में तो थकते कैसे
नक़्श[2] के बाद नये नक़्श निखारे हमने
की ये दीवार बलंद, और बलंद, और बलंद
बामो-दर[3] और ज़रा और सँवारे हमने

आँधियाँ तोड़ लिया करती थी शम्ओं की लवें
जड़ दिये इसलिये बिजली के सितारे हमने
बन गया क़स्र[4] तो पहरे पे कोई बैठ गया
सो रहे खाक पं हम शोरिशे-तामीर[5] लिये

अपनी नस-नस में लिये मेहनत-ए-पैहम[6] की थकन
बन्द आँखों में इसी क़स्र की तस्वीर लिये
दिन पिघलता है इसी तरह सरों पर अब तक
रात आँखों में खटकती है सियह तीर लिये

---

1. मकान में रहने वाले, 2. आकृति, 3. छत और दरवाज़े 4. महल 5. निर्माण का
कोलाहल, 6. निरंतर श्रम।

House

Tonight a searingly hot breeze is blowing,
Tonight on this footpath there will be no sleep
Come let us arise, you and I, and you too, and you
A window in this wall will surely find an opening.

To swallow us this earth was even then waiting
When our feet touched the ground from branches breaking
These houses know nothing, those who live in them
Know nothing of the days we spent in caves hiding.

Our hands could not tire, they had become the mould
To make statue after statue for someone else to hold
We made the wall strong, stronger and stronger still
Embellished the roof, gave doorways a strength untold.

Because the wind could so easily extinguish the flame
We gilded the sky with electricity instead
When the palace was built, someone else sat on guard
In squalor we slept with cacophony our bed.

The fatigue of relentless labour in every vein
Images of the palace in our eyes remain
Unending, the day melts on our heads still
Our unslept nights remain just the same.

आज की रात बहुत गर्म हवा चलती है
आज की रात न फुटपाथ पे नींद आयेगी
सब उठो, मैं भी उठूँ, तुम भी उठो, तुम भी उठो
कोई खिड़की इसी दीवार में खुल जायेगी

Tonight a searingly hot breeze is blowing,
Tonight on this footpath there will be no sleep
Come let us arise, you and I, and you too, and you
A window in this wall will surely find an opening.

मेरा माज़ी¹ मेरे कांधे पर

अब तमद्दुन² की हो ये जीत कि हार
मेरा माज़ी है अभी तक मेरे कांधे प सवार
आज भी दौड़ के गले मैं जो मिल जाता हूँ
जाग उठता है मेरे सीने में जंगल कोई
सींग माथे प उभर आते हैं।

पड़ता रहता है मेरे माज़ी का साया³ मुझ पर
दौरे-खूँख़ारी⁴ से गुज़रा हूँ छुपाऊं क्यूँ कर
दाँत सब खून में डूबे नज़र आते हैं।

जिन से मेरा न कोई बैर न प्यार
उन प करता हूँ मैं वार⁵
उन का करता हूँ शिकार
और भरता हूँ जनम अपना

पेट से मेरा जिस्म है दिल है न दिमाग़
कितने अवतार बढ़े लेके हथेली प चिराग़
देखते रह गये धो पाये न माज़ी का ये दाग़

---

1. अतीत. 2. संस्कृति. 3. छाया. 4. रक्तपात से भरा युग 5. आक्रमण

My Past Sits Heavy on My Shoulder

Whether it is culture's victory or loss
My past sits heavy on my shoulder even now
Even today when I join a herd of beasts
A jungle comes alive on my chest
And horns sprout from my forehead.

The shadow of my past keeps falling on me
Centuries of bloodletting, why should I hide?
My teeth appear to be immersed in blood.

Those whom I neither hate nor love
I hunt them
I pounce on them
And yield to the corporeal lust for survival.

My body is only stomach, not mind or heart
Many incarnations with a torch held aloft
Have failed to wash this stain of the past.

मल लिया माथे प तहज़ीब[6] का ग़ाज़ा[7] लेकिन
बरबरीयत[8] का जो है दाग़ वो छूटा ही नहीं
गाँव आबाद किये शहर बसाये हम ने
रिश्ता जंगल से जो अपना है वो टूटा ही नहीं
जब किसी मोड़ प पर खोल के उड़ता है गुबार
और नज़र आता है उसमें कोई मासूम शिकार
जाने क्यूँ हो जाता है जुनूँ एक सवार

किसी झाड़ी से उलझ के जो कभी टूटी थी
वही दुम फिर से निकल आती है
अपनी टाँगों में दबा के जिसे भरता हूँ ज़क़ंद[9]
इतना गिर जाता हूँ सदियों में हुवा जितना बुलन्द

अब तमद्दुन की हो ये जीत के हार
मेरा माज़ी है अभी तक मेरे कांधे प सवार।

---

6. सभ्यता, 7. पाउडर, 8. पशुता, 9. छलांग लगाना।

We rubbed the powder of culture on our forehead
But the stain of barbarity refused to go,
We established villages, settled homes
But the relationship with the jungle refused to go,
When the dust cloud opens its wings to fly
And within it can be seen an innocent victim
Don't know why an obsession takes over us.

The same tail, which rubbing against a bush
Had broken off, begins to sprout again
Tucking it between my legs, I leap
And fall as low as for centuries I had risen.

Whether it is culture's victory or its loss
My past sits heavy on my shoulder even now.

एक लम्हा[1]

ज़िन्दगी नाम है कुछ लम्हों का
और उन में भी वही इक लम्हा
जिसमें दो बोलती आँखें
चाय की प्याली से जब उट्ठें
तो दिल में डूबें
डूब के दिल में कहें
आज तुम कुछ न कहो
आज मैं कुछ न कहूँ
बस यूहीं बैठे रहो
हाथ में हाथ लिये
ग़म की सौग़ात लिये
गर्मी-ए-जज्बात[2] लिये
कौन जाने कि इसी लम्हे में
दूर परबत पे कहीं
बर्फ़ पिघलने ही लगे

---

1. क्षण, 2. भावनाओं की गर्मी।

A Moment in Time

Life is the name given to a few moments, and
In but one of those fleeting moments
Two eyes meet eloquently
Looking up from a cup of tea, and
Enter the heart piercingly
And say,
Today do not speak
I'll be silent too
Let's just sit thus.
Holding each other's hand
United by this gift of sorrow
Bonded by the stirring of emotions.
Who knows if in this very moment
Somewhere in the distant mountain
The snow at last may start to thaw.

पहला सलाम

एक चंचल झिझक, एक अल्हड़ पयाम[1]
हाय 'कैफ़ी' किसी का वह पहला सलाम

फूल रुख़सार[2] के रसमसाने लगे
हाथ उट्ठा क़दम डगमगाने लगे

रंग सा ख़ालो-ख़द[3] से छलकने लगा
सर से रंगीन आँचल ढलकने लगा

अजनबीयत निगाहें चुराने लगी
दिल धड़कने लगा, लहर आने लगी

साँस में इक गुलाबी गिरह पड़ गयी
होंट थरराये, सिमटे, नज़र गड़ गयी

रह गया उम्र भर के लिए यह हिजाब[4]
क्यों न सँभला हुआ दे सका मैं जवाब

क्यों मैं बे-क़स्द[5], बे-अज़्म[6], बे-वास्ता[7]
दूसरी सिम्त घबरा के तकने लगा

---

1. सन्देश. 2. गाल, 3. सुन्दर मुखड़ा (ख़ाल-काला तिल;-ख़द गाल) 4. संकोच,
5. अनायास, 6. बिना किसी इरादे के, 7. निरीह भाव से।

First Meeting

A mischievous restraint, a glance of seduction
Such was her greeting, 'Kaifi', on that first occasion.

The glow on her cheeks was like flowers in ferment
A hand half-raised, the feet uncertain.

Colour seemed to splash from her lovely countenance
From her head slipped the veil in obvious torment.

The eyes seemed to feign a lack of recognition
The heart began to pound in helpless confusion.

The breath was caught in a pink-hued constriction
Lips fluttered but stilled, the eyes fixed in exclusion.

What remained for a life was this strange hesitation
Why did my response lack that confident assertion.

Why did I suddenly, without wanting to, feigning indifference
Look away from her in some other direction.

ग़ज़ल

मैं ढूँढता हूँ जिसे वह जहाँ नहीं मिलता
नयी ज़मीन नया आसमाँ नहीं मिलता

नयी ज़मीन नया आसमाँ भी मिल जाये
नये बशर¹ का कहीं कुछ निशाँ नहीं मिलता

वह तेग़² मिल गयी जिससे हुआ है क़त्ल मेरा
किसी के हाथ का उस पर निशाँ नहीं मिलता

वह मेरा गाँव है वो मेरे गाँव के चूल्हे
कि जिनमें शोले तो शोले, धुँआ नहीं मिलता

जो इक खुदा नहीं मिलता तो इतना मातम क्या
मुझे खुद अपने क़दम का निशाँ नहीं मिलता

खड़ा हूँ कबसे मैं चेहरों के एक जंगल में
तुम्हारे चेहरे का कुछ भी यहाँ नहीं मिलता

---

1. मानव, 2. तलवार।

14

Ghazal

The world I seek I cannot find
A new earth, a new sky I cannot find.

A new earth, a new sky even if I found
No trace of a new man can I find.

I have found the dagger that was used to slay me
No one's fingerprints on it can I find.

That is my village, those my village hearths
Let alone the embers, smoke I cannot find.

It is no great calamity if God cannot be found
A trace of my own footprints I cannot find.

For an eternity I have stood here among the crowd
Not a trace of your face can I find.

पशेमानी[1]

मैं यह सोचकर उसके दर से उठा था
कि वह रोक लेगी, मना लेगी मुझको

हवाओं में लहराता आता था दामन
कि दामन पकड़कर बिठा लेगी मुझको

क़दम ऐसे अंदाज़ से उठ रहे थे
कि आवाज़ देकर बुला लेगी मुझको

मगर उसने रोका न मुझको मनाया
न दामन ही पकड़ा न मुझको बिठाया

न आवाज़ ही दी, न वापस बुलाया
मैं आहिस्ता-आहिस्ता बढ़ता ही आया

यहाँ तक कि उससे जुदा हो गया मैं

---

1. शर्मिन्दगी, पछतावा।

16

A Sense of Regret

When from her doorway I stood up to go,
I thought she would cajole me and make me stay,

The wind billowed my garment towards her
I thought she would seize it and request me to stay,

My footsteps moved away so reluctantly from her
I thought she would call out and ask me to stay,

Truth is, she did not stop me, nor sought to cajole me
She caught not my garment, nor tried to delay me

She broke not her silence, nor moved to address me
I kept walking slowly on,

Ever so slowly I kept walking away, so far that we are
                                        separated today.

लखनऊ तो नहीं

अज़ा[1] में बहते थे आँसू यहाँ लहू तो नहीं,
ये कोई और जगह होगी लखनऊ तो नहीं।

यहाँ तो चलती हैं छुरयाँ ज़बान से पहले,
ये मीर 'अनीस' की, 'आतश' की गुफ़्तगू तो नहीं।

टपक रहा है जो ज़ख़्मों से दोनों फ़िरक़ों[2] के,
बग़ौर देखो ये इस्लाम का लहू तो नहीं।

तुम इसका रख लो कोई और नाम मौजूँ-सा,[3]
किया है खून से जो तूमने वो वज़ू तो नहीं।

बुझा रहे हैं जिसे आप अपने दामन से,
कहीं वो आप ही की शम्अ-ए-आरज़ू तो नहीं।

समझ के माल मेरा जिसको तुमने लूटा है,
पड़ोसियों! वो तुम्हारी ही आबरू तो नहीं।

---

1. शोक, 2. सम्प्रदायों 3. उपयुक्त-सा।

18

Lucknow Could It Be?

Tears have flowed here in sorrow, but never blood,
This must be some other place, or Lucknow could it be?

Here knives move faster than tongues can aspire,
The language of Mir 'Anees' and 'Atash' could it be?

The blood that drips from the wounds of both communities,
Examine it carefully, Islam's blood could it be?

Give it any name that you consider apt,
What you have done in blood, ablution could it be?

This that you extinguish with your own garment,
The flame of your dreams for the morrow could it be?

All you have looted thinking it mine,
O neighbours, your honour could it be?

दोपहर

ये जीत-हार तो इस दौर का मुक़द्दर है
ये दौर जो कि पुराना नहीं नया भी नहीं
ये दौर जो कि सज़ा भी नहीं जज़ा[1] भी नहीं
ये दौर जिसका बज़ाहिर कोई ख़ुदा भी नहीं

तुम्हारी जीत अहम[2] है न मेरी हार अहम
कि इब्तिदा[3] भी नहीं है, ये इन्तिहा[4] भी नहीं
शुरू मारिका-ए-जाँ अभी हुआ ही नहीं
शुरू हो तो ये हंगामे-फ़ैसला[6] भी नहीं

पयामे-ज़ेर-ए-लब[7] अब तक है सूरे-इसराफ़ील[8]
सुना किसी ने किसी ने अभी सुना भी नहीं
किया किसी ने किसी ने यक़ी किया भी नहीं
उठा ज़मीन से कोई, कोई उठा भी नहीं

ये कारवाँ है तो अंजामे-कारवाँ[9] मालूम
कि अजनबी भी नहीं कोई कोई आशना[10] भी नहीं
किसी से ख़ुश भी नहीं है कोई ख़फ़ा भी नहीं
किसी का हाल कोई मुड़ के पूछता भी नहीं

---

1. पुण्यफल, उपकार, 2. महत्वपूर्ण, 3. आदि, आरंभ, 4. अंत, 5. जान की लड़ाई,
6. निर्णय का क्षण, 7. दबे स्वर में दिया गया संदेश, 8. प्रलय-घोष (क़यामत के समय
इस्राफ़ील फ़रिश्ता सूर फूँकेंगा), 9. कारवाँ का परिणाम, 10. परिचित।

Afternoon

Victory or defeat is the fate of this journey
A journey not new nor of great antiquity,
This journey which is neither punishment nor reward
This journey which is bereft of a God.

Your victory is insignificant, my defeat inconsequential
This is neither a beginning nor an ending that is final,
The struggle for survival has not yet begun
Then why this furore for a final decision?

Like a silent whisper comes the news of calamity
Did someone hear or was it unheard entirely?
A few were believers but nobody believed
A few rose from the ground some remained unredeemed.

If this be the caravan its fate is known
No one is either a stranger, or entirely known,
None is pleased with another, nor is angry
None pauses to ask if the other is unhappy.

ग़ज़ल

बस एक झिझक है यही हाले-दिल सुनाने में
कि तेरा ज़िक्र भी आयेगा इस फ़साने में

बरस पड़ी थी जो रूख़ से नक़ाब उठाने में
वो चाँदनी है अभी तब ग़रीबख़ाने में

उसी में इश्क़ की क़िस्मत बदल भी सकती थी
जो वक़्त बीत गया मुझको आज़माने में

ये कहके टूट गया शाख़े-गुल से आख़िरी फूल
अब और देर है कितनी बहार आने में

Ghazal

Only one thought stops me from speaking my heart
That you too would figure in it at least in part.

The moonrays that enveloped me when you raised your veil
Still shed their lustre on my lonely trail.

Perhaps love's fate can change altogether
In the time that you spend judging my ardour.

The last flower fell while wanting to know
How long must it wait for spring's glorious glow.

दायरा

रोज़ बढ़ता हूँ जहाँ से आगे
फिर वहीं लौट के आ जाता हूँ
बारहा तोड़ चुका हूँ जिनको
उन्हीं दीवारों से टकराता हूँ
रोज़ बसते हैं क़ई शहर नये
रोज़ धरती में समा जाते हैं
जलज़लों[1] में थी ज़रा सी गर्मी
वो भी अब रोज़ ही आ जाते हैं
जिस्म से रूह तलक रेत ही रेत
न कहीं धूप, न साया, न सराब[2]
कितने अरमान हैं किस सहरा[3] में
कौन रखता है मज़ारों[4] का हिसाब
नब्ज़ बुझती भी भड़कती भी है
दिल का मामूल[5] है घबराना भी
रात अँधेरे ने अँधेरे से कहा
एक आदत है जिये जाना भी
कौस[6] इक रंग की होती है तुलूअ[7]
एक ही चाल भी पैमाने की
गोशे-गोशे[8] में खड़ी है मस्जिद
शक्ल क्या हो गयी मैख़ाने की

---

1. भूकंपों, 2. मृगतृष्णा, 3. मरुस्थल, 4. कब्रों 5. स्वाभाविक आचरण, 6. इन्द्रधनुष,
7. उदय, 8. कौने-कौने

Circle

Everyday from where I go ahead
I come back to the same spot again,
The walls I have broken so many times
Are the walls I strike all over again,
Everyday new towns come into being
Everyday the earth subsumes them again,
Earthquakes at least had a heat of their own
Now they just recur over and again.
From the body to the soul an endless desert
No sun, no mirage, no shade,
So many hopes have perished in the desert waste
Who cares a damn for the grave,
The pulse dies and flutters again
The heart's natural attribute is anxiety,
At night the night whispered to itself
To go on living is a habit in itself.
A rainbow is a bouquet of but one colour
A goblet has its own trajectory,
If mosques begin to stand at every corner
What can the shape of the tavern be?

कोई कहता था समंदर हूँ मैं
और मेरी जेब में क़तरा भी नहीं
ख़ैरियत अपनी लिखा करता हूँ
अब तो तक़दीर में ख़तरा भी नहीं
अपने हाथों को पढ़ा करता हूँ
कभी कुरआँ[9], कभी गीता की तरह
चंद रेखाओं में सीमाओं में
ज़िंदगी क़ैद है सीता की तरह
राम कब लौटेंगे, मालूम नहीं
काश रावण ही कोई आ जाता

---

9. कुरान।

Somebody used to say he is the ocean itself
When not even a drop was with me,
Now I write to all that I'm fine
Now danger too is absent from my destiny,
I read the lines on my palm
Like I would the Koran or the Gita,
In the confines of a few lines
My life is imprisoned like Sita,
When Rama will return I cannot say
If only some Ravana would come and stay.

ग़ज़ल

सुना करो मेरी जाँ इनसे उनसे अफ़साने
सब अजनबी हैं यहाँ कौन किसको पहचाने

यहाँ से जल्द गुज़र जाओ क़ाफ़िले वालो!
हैं मेरी प्यास के फूंके हुए ये वीराने

मेरे जुनूने-परस्तिश¹ से तंग आ गये लोग
सुना है बन्द किये जा रहे हैं बुतख़ाने²

जहाँ से पिछले पहर कोई तश्नाकाम³ उठा
वहीं पे तोड़े हैं यारों ने आज पैमाने

बहार आये तो मेरा सलाम कह देना
मुझे तो आज तलब कर लिया है सहरा⁴ ने

हुआ है हुक्म कि 'कैफ़ी' को संगसार⁵ करो
मसीह⁶ बैठे हैं छुप के कहाँ ख़ुदा जाने

---

1. उपासना का उन्माद 2. उपासनागृह, मंदिर, 3. प्यासा, 4. मरुस्थल, 5. पत्थर से मारना, 6, ईसा, जिन्होंने आदेश दिया था कि पहला पत्थर वह मारे जिसने स्वयं कोई पाप न किया हो।

Ghazal

Listen, my love, to the stories they all tell,
Everyone's a stranger here, no one the other knows.

Pass by this place quickly, O caravan travellers,
Singed by my thirst, in this barrenness nothing grows.

People have had enough of my tempestuous worship
I hear that even temples are being asked to close.

From where someone thirsty left but a while ago
There friends revel today, and wine overflows.

If spring comes, do give it my salaam
I am now a part of what the desert chose.

An order has been passed that 'Kaifi' should be stoned
Where hides the saviour, alas, only God knows.

हौसला

तू ख़ुरशीद[1] है बादलों में न छुप
तू महताब[2] है जगमगाना न छोड़

तू शोख़ी है शोख़ी, रिआयत न कर
तू बिजली है बिजली, जलाना न छोड़

अभी इश्क़ ने हार मानी नहीं
अभी इश्क़ को आज़माना न छोड़

---

1. सूरज, 2. चाँद।

Courage

You are the sun, don't hide in the clouds
You are the moon, continue to shine.

You are mischievous seduction, don't let it subside
You are the lightning, continue to strike.

Love has not yet admitted defeat
Continue to test it, as much as you like.

ग़ज़ल

वो कभी धूप कभी छाँव लगे
मुझे क्या क्या न मेरा गाँव लगे

किसी पीपल के तले जा बैठें
अब भी अपना जो कोई दाँव लगे

एक रोटी के तआक्क़ुब[1] में चला हूँ इतना
कि मेरा पाँव किसी और ही का पाँव लगे

रोटी-रोज़ी की तलब जिसको कुचल देती है
उस की ललकार भी इक सहमी हुई म्याँव लगे

जैसे देहात में लू लगती है चरवाहों को
बम्बई में यूँही तारों की हसीं छाँव लगे

---

1. पीछा करना।

Ghazal

Often like the sun and sometimes the shade
My village for me has a hundred shapes.

To sit under the shade of a peepal tree
O, if I had a chance, I'd do that gladly.

In pursuit of bread I have walked many miles
My feet no longer feel like mine.

He who is crushed by the hunger for daily bread
As subdued as a cat's hushed mewling is his protest.

The beautiful shade of stars in Bombay feels the same
As the hot winds that sear the cowherd on a burning day.

ग़ज़ल

पत्थर के ख़ुदा वहाँ भी पाये
हम चाँद से आज लौट आये

दीवारें तो हर तरफ़ खड़ी हैं
क्या हो गये मेहरबान[1] साये

जंगल की हवाएँ आ रही हैं
काग़ज़ का ये शहर उड़ न जाये

लैला ने नया जनम लिया है
है क़ैस[2] कोई जो दिल लगाये

है आज ज़मीं का ग़ुस्ले-सेहत[3]
जिस दिल में हो जितना ख़ून लाये

सहरा-सहरा[4] लहू के ख़ेमे
फिर प्यासे लब-ए-फ़रात[5] आये

---

1. कृपालु, 2. मजनूं, 3. स्वास्थ्य-लाभ के बाद पहला स्नान, 4. हर मरुस्थल में,
5. फ़रात नदी के किनारे।

Ghazal

Even there, the gods were of stone
The moon from where we returned today.

Walls loom tall all around
Where have the merciful shadows gone?

A strong wind from the jungle is blowing our way
These towns of paper cannot stay.

Laila has been born again
Is there a Qais who can dare to be obsessed with her again?

Today the earth will be washed anew
Let each give blood as their hearts dictate.

Deserts simmer under the awning of blood
To the Farat riverbanks the thirsty returns again.

मशविरे

पीरी:

'यह आँधी, यह तूफ़ान, ये तेज़ धारे
कड़कते तमाशे, गरजते नज़ारे
अँधेरी फ़ज़ा, साँस लेता समंदर
न हमराह मिशअल[1], न गर्दूँ[2] पे तारे
मुसाफ़िर, खड़ा रहा अभी जी को मारे'

शबाब:

'उसी का है साहिल, उसी के कगारे
तलातुम[3] में फँसकर जो दो हाथ मारे
अँधेरी फ़ज़ा, साँस लेता समंदर
यूँहीं सर पटकते रहेंगे ये धारे
कहाँ तक चलेगा किनारे-किनारे'

---

1. मशाल, 2. आकाश, 3. बाढ़, तूफ़ान।

Advice

Age:

'This wind, this storm, this furious flow
This thunder and lightning, this frightening show
The night is dark, the ocean heaves
No torch to guide, or star aglow
Traveller, stay where you are, fight not this flow.'

Youth:

'For him is the guide, for him the shore
Who fights the flood without awaiting the oar
The pitch-dark night, the heaving ocean
Are but a whimper in comparison to resolve's roar
How long can you walk clinging to the shore?'

दो रातें

उलझे–उलझे हुए जज़्बात न पूछ
सहमी–सहमी सी इनायात[1] न पूछ
बार–बार उसका करम[2] फ़रमाना
चुपके–चुपके सरे–बालीं[3] आना
जाने क्या–क्या वो मुझे समझाना
और फिर आप ही शरमा जाना
मुख़्तसर[4] कितनी थी वो रात न पूछ

आह ममनूने–असर[5] हो कि न हो
देखिये रात बसर हो कि न हो
अब्र[6] उजड़े हुए मँडलाये हुए
तौर[7] सहमे हुए घबराये हुए
अश्क[8] रुख़्सार[9] पे कुछ आये हुए
और कुछ पलकों में थर्राये हुए
अब ख़ुदा जाने सहर हो कि न हो

---

1. कृपाएँ, 2. कृपालुता, 3. सिराहने, 4. छोटी, 5. प्रभाव की आभारी, प्रभावशाली,
6. बादल, 7. आचरण, 8. आँसू, 9. गाल।

Two Nights

Ask not how confused my thoughts are
Or why my kindness is so subdued.
Again and again her willingness to give,
To arrive at my bed, furtive and scared
Wanting to explain who knows what to me
Then being overcome with shyness, suddenly.
How short that night was, O do not ask.

Whether this yearning fulfils, or not
Whether this night passes, or not
The clouds are scattered, ready to dissolve
The mood is tense, unwilling to resolve
A tear or two is visible on the cheek
Or caught in the lashes awaiting release
Now God alone knows whether the dawn will break, or not.

ग़ज़ल

लायी फिर इक लग़्ज़िशे-मस्ताना[1] तेरे शहर में
फिर बनेंगी मस्जिदें मैख़ाना तेरे शहर में

आज फिर टूटेंगी तेरे घर की नाज़ुक खिड़कियाँ
आज फिर देखा गया दीवाना तेरे शहर में

जुर्म है तेरी गली से सर झुकाकर लौटना
कुफ़्र[2] है पथराव से घबराना तेरे शहर में

शाहनामे[3] लिख्खे हैं खँडरात की हर ईंट पर
हर जगह है दफ़्न इक अफ़साना तेरे शहर में

कुछ कनीज़ें[4] जो हरीमे-नाज़[5] में हैं बारयाब[6]
माँगती हैं जानो-दिल नज़राना तेरे शहर में

नंगी सड़कों पर भटककर देख, जब मरती है रात
रेंगता है हर तरफ़ वीराना तेरे शहर में

---

1. मादक लड़खड़ाहट, 2. विधर्मिता, सिद्धान्त के विरुद्ध, 3. फ़िरदौसी की अमर कृति,
4. दासियाँ, 5. प्रेमिका का घर, 6. जिसे प्रवेश मिल गया हो।

Ghazal

That drunken step once again brings me to your town
Mosques once again will be taverns in your town.

The delicate windows of your home will once again break
A lunatic once again has been seen in your town.

It is a crime to return, head bowed, from your street
It is blasphemy to fear being stoned in your town.

The *Shahnama* is written on every brick of this ruin
Everywhere a story lies buried in your town.

The maids who have access to the beloved's home
Ask for one's life and heart as a token in your town.

When, on a naked street, the night breathes its last
Then watch how desolation crawls about in your town.

इंतशार

कभी जमूद' कभी सिर्फ़ इंतशार² –सा है
जहाँ को अपनी तबाही का इंतज़ार–सा है
मनु की मछली, न कशती ए–नूह और ये फ़ज़ा
कि क़तरे–क़तरे में तूफ़ान बेक़रार–सा है
तमाम जिस्म है बेदार,³ फ़िक्र ख़ाबीदा⁴
दिमाग़ पिछले ज़माने की यादगार–सा है
सब अपने पाँव पे रख–रखके पाँव चलते हैं
ख़ुद अपने दोश⁵ पे हर आदमी सवार–सा है
जिसे पुकारिये मिलता है इक खँडहर से जवाब
जिसे भी देखिये माज़ी⁶ का इश्तहार–सा है
हुई तो कैसे बियाबाँ ⁷ में आके शाम हुई
कि जो मज़ार यहाँ है मेरा मज़ार–सा है
कोई तो सूद चुकाये, कोई तो ज़िम्मा ले
उस इन्क़लाब का, जो आज तक उधार–सा है

---

1. गतिरोध, 2. बिखराव, अस्त-व्यस्त होना, 3. जागा हुआ, 4. सोयी हुई. 5. कंधा, 6. अतीत, 7. वन।

Dispersion

Sometimes an obstruction, sometimes a dispersion
The world perhaps awaits its own destruction.
Not Manu's fish, nor Noah's Ark, but just this dread,
Each drop seems to be a storm waiting to break ahead.
The body fully alert, the intellect unawake
The mind seems a shadow lost in memory's wake.
We walk in each other's footsteps without leaving a trace
Astride our own shoulders we move from place to place.
Ruins echo an answer, whoever we call
The past seems to hold each one in thrall.
The sun had to set in that very wilderness
Where the tomb bears to mine a strange likeness.
Someone must pay the price , someone must bear the blame
Of the revolution that even today is a borrowed claim.

ग़ज़ल

की है कोई हसीन ख़ता हर ख़ता के साथ,
थोड़ा-सा प्यार भी मुझे दे दो सज़ा के साथ।

गर डूबना ही अपना मुक़द्दर है तो सुनो,
डूबेंगे हम ज़रूर मगर नाख़ुदा[1] के साथ।

मंज़िल से वो भी दूर था और हम भी दूर थे,
हमने भी धूल उड़ायी बहुत रहनुमा[2] के साथ।

रक़्से-सबा[3] के जश्न[4] में हम तुम भी नाचते,
ऐ काश तुम भी आ गये होते सबा के साथ।

ऐसा लगा ग़रीबी की रेखा से हूँ बलन्द[5]
पूछा किसी ने हाल कुछ ऐसी अदा के साथ।

---

1. खेवनहार, माँझी, 2. मार्ग दर्शक, 3. पुरवाई का नृत्य, 4. उत्सव, 5. ऊँचा।

Ghazal

With all my mistakes there's always a sweet one too,
Along with my punishment, O, give me a little love too.

If my destiny is to drown, then this too is true,
Drown I surely will, but take the boatman with me too.

For from the destination was he and far from it were we
Directionless walked the torch-bearer, and along with him
walked we.

You could have danced with me in the east wind's whirling
form,
If only you were willing to be carried by the storm.

For a moment I felt well above the poverty line
When someone asked with great style, 'Hey, mister, are you
fine?'

पुरसुकून[1] समंदर

ऐ थके हारे समंदर तू मचलता क्यों नहीं
तू उछलता क्यों नहीं।

साहिलों[2] को तोड़ के बाहर निकलता क्यों नहीं
तू मचलता क्यों नहीं
तू उछलता क्यों नहीं।

तेरे साहिल पर सितम की बस्तियाँ आबाद हैं
शहर के मेमार[3] सारे ख़ानमाँ-बरबाद[4] हैं
ऐसी काली बस्तियों को तू निगलता क्यों नहीं
तू उछलता क्यों नहीं
तू मचलता क्यों नहीं।

तुझ में लहरें हैं न मौजें हैं न शोर
ज़ुल्म से बेज़ार दुनियाँ देखती है तेरी ओर
तू उबलता क्यों नहीं
तू उछलता क्यों नहीं
तू मचलता क्यों नहीं।

ऐ थके हारे समंदर तू मचलता क्यों नहीं
तू उछलता क्यों नहीं।

---

1. शांत, 2. तटों, 3. घर बनाने वाले, 4. जिनका घर बरबाद हो।

Tranquil Ocean

O, Ocean, overwhelmed by defeat and fatigue
Why do you not seethe?
Why do you not rage?

Why do you not overpower your shores
Why do you not rise?
Why do you not rage?

Exploiters' settlements deface your shores
The homes of builders are dens of vice
Why do you not swallow such settlements of shame
Why do you not seethe?
Why do you not rage?

You have no waves, no crest, no fury
The wretched of this earth watch you silently
Why do you not seethe?
Why do you not foam?
Why do you not rage?

O, Ocean, overwhelmed by defeat and fatigue
Why do you not seethe?
Why do you not rage?

आईना

आईना तोड़ दिया, तोड़ दिया, तोड़ दिया
शक्ल एक बार ज़रा देख तो लो
देखो, अब कैसी नज़र आती हो
फिर वही आँखों में रंग आता है
या झिझक जाती हो, डर जाती हो

इसी आईने में देखा था वो हुस्न
जिसका दुश्वार' यक़ीं होता है
और पूछा था बड़े नाज़ के साथ
कोई इतना भी हसीं होता है

इसमें आईने की खूबी तो नहीं
हुस्न जब था तो नज़र आया था
पा चुकी थी तुम्हें दुनिया लेकिन
तुमने अपने को कहाँ पाया था

ओर जब अपने को पाया तुमने
जाने आईने को क्यों तोड़ दिया
हादसा' ये भी नहीं है लेकिन
देखना अपने को क्यों छोड़ दिया

शक्ल एक बार ज़रा देख तो लो
देखो, अब कैसी नज़र आती हो

---

1. कठिन, 2. दुर्घटना।

Mirror

You have broken the mirror,
Look at your face but once
See how you look now
Do your eyes flash like they once did?
Or do you hesitate and turn away scared?

In this very mirror I saw a beauty
That was hard to believe,
I had asked with great pride
Can anyone be as beautiful as she?

There was nothing unique in the mirror
The beauty was there, it was there to see,
But the world had already discovered you
Only you had not made your own discovery.

And when you found yourself
Who knows why you broke the mirror,
This in itself was of no consequence
But why did you stop seeing your own reflection?

See yourself just once more
See now, how you appear.

दस्तूरे-बख़्शिश[1]

लबालब हैं कहीं सागर, कहीं ख़ाली पियाले हैं
ये कैसा दौर हे साक़ी, ये क्या तक़्सीम है साक़ी

नहीं पहचानता तेवर अभी तू तिश्नाकामों[2] के
तेरा दस्तूरे-बख़्शिश लायक़े-तरमीम[3] है साक़ी

---

1. दान-पद्धति, 2. प्यासों, 3. बदलने योग्य।

The Custom of Giving

For some, the cups overflow, for some they remain empty
Are these rounds for show, or, is the division fair, O saki?

You do not know yet the mien of the thirsty
Your manner of giving must change, O saki.

नज़्रे जाफ़री

अली सरदार जाफ़री की 70वीं सालगिरह पर

रहे जो रहता है बेज़ार[1] बाग़बाँ[2] तुझसे
बहार तुझसे, सबा तुझसे, गुलिस्ताँ तुझसे

सुकूते-ग़म[3] को मिली जुर्ते-बयाँ[4] तुझसे
कलाम तुझसे, सुख़न[5] तुझसे, दास्ताँ[6] तुझसे

हर एक सफ़्हा-ए-किरतास[7] गुलिस्ताँ तुझसे
हर एक बुलबुले-तस्वीर[8] नग़्माख़ाँ[9] तुझसे

नजूम[10] तुझसे महो-महरो-कहकशाँ[11] तुझसे
हुई ज़मीने-सुख़न[12] रश्के-आसमाँ[13] तुझसे

बहुत सुबुक[14] थी तराज़ूए-शेर[15] तुझसे
ख़ुशा[16] कि आज है पल्ला बहुत गराँ[17] तुझसे[18]

फ़ज़ा-ए-तीरा[19] में जुगनू तेरे तरानों के
हर एक क़तरए-शबनम शरर फ़शाँ[20] तुझसे

---

1. विरक्त, 2. माली, 3. दुख की शांति, 4. कहने का साहस, 5. कविता, 6. कथा,
7. कागज का पन्ना, 8. बुलबुल का चित्र, 9. संगीतज्ञ, 10. नक्षत्र, 11. चन्द्र व सूर्य
व आकाश गंगा, 12. कविता भूमि, 13. जिस पर आकाश ईर्ष्या करे, 14. सुबुक,
15. कविता की तुला, 16. मुबारक बाद, 17. भारी, 18. यह शेर मीर अनीस के
निम्नलिखित शेर पर आधारित है:

> सुबुक हो चली थी तराज़ू-ए-शेर
> मगर हमने पल्ला गराँ कर दिया।

19. अँधेरा वातावरण 20. आग उगलता हुआ।

For Jafri

For Ali Sardar Jafri on his seventieth birthday

Even if the gardener is indifferent to you
The spring, the breeze, the bouquet come from you.

Numb sorrow is given a voice by you
The writing, the poetry, the story come from you.

Every blank page is splashed with colours by you
Every picture of a bulbul begins to sing through you.

The constellations are yours, the milky way is brought alive
                                                     through you
The skies look on with envy when poetry flows from you.

The scale of poetry had once found a balance because of you
Felicitations, the scale has now dipped towards you.

Like glow-worms at night, your hymns illumine the dark
Each drop of morning dew sparkles like fire because of you.

फ़ज़ा[21] में तूने बिखेरे हैं इंक़्लाब के गीत
दयारे-गाँधी[22] में लेनिन की 'दास्ताँ' तुझसे

रुमूज़ हिकमते-इक़बाल[23] तूने समझाए
हुआ है इश्क़ का सिर्रे-निहाँ[24] अयाँ[25] तुझसे

तुझे चमन में कहीं आशियाँ[26] मिले न मिले
चली रवायते-तामीरे-आशियाँ[27] तुझसे

गुलाम हो वो या स्वतंत्र भारत हो,
ख़फ़ा ख़फ़ा रहे दोनों के हुक्मराँ[28] तुझसे।

वो आज ढूँढते फिरते हैं तेरे नक़्शे-क़दम,[29]
गुज़र रहे थे जो कल तक कशाँ-कशाँ[30] तुझसे।

बस इस दुआ पे ग़ज़ल ये तमाम होती है,
यूँही सजी रहे ये बज़्मे-दोस्ताँ तुझसे।

क़रीब इतना हूँ तुझसे कि कहना मुश्किल है,
मैं ज़िंदगी में मिला हूँ कहाँ-कहाँ तुझसे।

---

21. वातावरण 22. गांधी के देश, 23. इक़बाल के ज्ञान का रहस्य, 24. आन्तरिक रहस्य,
25. स्पष्ट, 26. घोसला, घर, 27. घोसला बनाने की परम्परा, 28. शासक, 29. पद
चिन्ह, 30. खिंचे-खिंचे।

54

You have spread all around the song of rebellion
In the land of Gandhi, Lenin's call resounds through you.

It was you who explained the mystery of Iqbal
Love's secrets too were revealed by you.

You may or may not build a nest for yourself
But the inspiration to build a nest comes from you.

Whether it is an India enslaved or independent
The rulers of both remained somewhat annoyed with you.

In search today for a sign of your footprints
Are those very people who kept a distance from you.

On this hope then this ghazal comes to a close
May this circle of friendship forever prosper through you.

So near am I to you that it's difficult to say
Where all in this long life I have met with you.

सोमनाथ

बुत-शिकन¹ कोई कहीं से भी न आने पाये
हमने कुछ बुत अभी सपने में सजा रक्खे हैं
अपने ख़ाबों में बसा रक्खे हैं

दिल पे ये सोच के पथराव करो दीवानो!
कि जहाँ हमने सनम² अपने छुपा रक्खे हैं
वहीं 'ग़ज़नी' के खुदा रक्खे हैं।

बुत जो टूटा तो किसी तरह बना लेंगे उन्हें
टुकड़े-टुकड़े सही दामन में उठा लेंगे उन्हें
फिर से उजड़े हुए सपने में सजा लेंगे उन्हें।

गर खुदा टूटेगा हम तो न बना पायेंगे
उसके बिखरे हुए टुकड़े न उठा पायेंगे
तुम उठा लो तो उठा लो शायद
तुम बना लो तो बना लो शायद।

तुम बनाओ तो खुदा जाने बनाओ कैसा
अपने जैसा ही बनाया तो क़यामत होगी
प्यार होगा न ज़माने में मुहब्बत होगी
दुश्मनी होगी अदावत³ होगी
हम से उसकी न इबादत होगी।

---

1. मूर्ति तोड़ने वाले, 2. मूर्ति, महबूब, 3. दुश्मनी।

Somnath

Let no idol destroyer come near
There are some idols we still hold dear
We have given them a home in our dreams.

Think this before you stone my heart, O heedless one,
That in the place where we have hidden our beloved
Ghazni has placed his own God.

If idols break, we can piece them together
Their shards embrace to our hearts
Adorn with them, once again, our broken dreams.

But if God breaks, we cannot put him together
His broken pieces cannot be gathered,
If you can pick them, then so be it
If you can make him, then so be it.

If you were to make God, who knows how you'd make him
If like yourself, it would be a calamity
The world will have neither love nor amity
There will be acrimony, no dearth of enmity
Such a God will not have our fealty.

वहशते-बुत शिकनी देख के हैराँ हूँ मैं,
बुत परस्ती मेरा शेवा' है कि इंसाँ हूँ मैं।
इक न इक बुत तो हर इक दिल में छुपा होता है।
उसके सौ नामों में इक नाम खुदा होता है।

---

4. स्वभाव

I am surprised at this frenzy of idol breaking
Idol breaking is my nature, for I am a human being.
Some idol or the other hides in every heart
Of its many names, one of them is God.

बहुरूपिनी

एक गर्दन पे सैकड़ों चेहरे
और हर चेहरे पर हज़ारों दाग़
और हर दाग़ बंद दरवाज़ा
रौशनी इनसे आ नहीं सकती
रौशनी इनसे जा नहीं सकती

जाने किस कोख ने जना इसको
जाने किस सहन¹ में जवान हुई
जाने किस देस से चली कमबख़्त
वैसे ये हर ज़बान बोलती है
ज़ख़्म खिड़की की तरह खोलती है

और कहती है झाँककर दिल में
तेरा मज़हब, तेरा अज़ीम² ख़ुदा
तेरी तहज़ीब³ के हसीन सनम⁴
सब को ख़तरे ने आज घेरा है
बाद उनके जहाँ अँधेरा है

सर्द हो जाता हे लहू मेरा
बंद हो जाती हैं खुली आँखें
ऐसा लगता है जैसे दुनिया में
सभी दुश्मन हैं कोई दोस्त नहीं
मुझको ज़िन्दा निगल रहीं है ज़मीं

---

1. आँगन. 2. महान्. 3. सभ्यता. 4. मूर्ति, महबूबा

Chameleon

On one neck, a million faces
On each face, a thousand scars
Each scar a closed door
Through which light cannot enter
Nor light go out.

Who knows which womb nurtured it?
Who knows where it grew up?
Who knows which country it came from?
In all the languages it knows how to speak
And opens wounds like a window's sweep.

And looking into my heart, it says:
Your religion, your great God
And the icons of your culture
Are all today in danger
Darkness looms beyond them.

My blood runs cold
My eyes close
It seems in this world
I have no friends, only enemies
And the earth is swallowing me alive.

ऐसा लगता है राक्षस कोई
एक गागर, कमर में लटकाकर
आसमाँ पर चढ़ेगा आख़िरे-शब[5]
नूर सारा निचोड़ लायेगा
मेरे तारे भी तोड़ लायेगा

ये जो धरती का फट गया सीना
और बाहर निकल पड़े हैं जलूस
मुझसे कहते हैं तुम हमारे हो
मैं अगर इनका हूँ, तो मैं क्या हूँ
मैं किसी का नहीं हूँ, अपना हूँ

मुझको तन्हाई ने दिया है जनम
मेरा सब कुछ अकेलेपन से है
कौन पूछेगा मुझको मेले में
साथ जिस दिन क़दम बढ़ाऊँगा
चाल मैं अपनी भूल जाऊँगा

ये और ऐसे ही चंद और सवाल
ढूँढने पर भी आज तक मुझको
जिनके माँ-बाप का मिला न सुराग़
ज़ेह्न में ये उँडेल देती है
मुझको मुट्ठी में भींच लेती है

चाहता हूँ कि क़त्ल कर दूँ इसे
वार लेकिन जब इस पे करता हूँ
मेरे सीने पे ज़ख़्म उभरते हैं
मेरे माथे से ख़ूँ टपकता है
जाने क्या मेरा इसका रिश्ता है

---

5. रात्रि का अंत, निशांत।

It seems that a demon
Armed with a pot at his waist
Will go up to the sky in the pitch-dark of the night
Will squeeze out all the joy of the light
Will pluck out even the stars that are mine.

Behold the earth split wide
Sprouting this procession of men
Who tell me I am theirs.
If I am theirs, who am I?
Not anyone's, I can only be mine.

Solitude gave birth to me
All I have stems from being alone
There is no one to search for me in a crowd
If I move once in tandem with you
I will forget my own way to walk.

It is questions like these
Whose answers I seek to find
To no avail, clueless, groping
It is such questions, arising in my mind
That leave me in a quagmire, sinking.

want to kill this thing
But whenever I attack it
Wounds break out on my chest
Blood drips from my forehead
I do not know how I am related to it.

आँधियों में अज़ान दी मैंने
शंख फूँका अँधेरी रातों में
घर के बाहर सलीब लटकायी
एक-इक दर से इसको ठुकराया
शहर से दूर जाके फेंक आया

और ऐलान कर दिया कि उठो
बर्फ़ सी जम गयी है सीनों पर
गर्म बोसों से इसको पिघला दो
कर लो जो भी गुनाह वो कम है
आज की रात जश्ने-आदम⁶ है

ये मेरी आस्तीन से निकली
रख दिया दौड़ के चिराग़ पे हाथ
मल दिया फिर अँधेरा चेहरे पर
होंठ से दिल की बात लौट गयी
दर तक आ के बारात लौट गयी

इसने मुझको अलग बुला के कहा
आज की ज़िन्दगी का नाम हे ख़ौफ़
ख़ौफ़ ही वो ज़मीन है जिसमें
फ़िरके⁷ उगते हैं, फ़िरक़े पलते हैं
धारे सागर से कटके चलते हैं

ख़ौफ़ जब तक दिलों में बाक़ी है
सिर्फ़ चेहरा बदलते रहना है
सिर्फ़ लहज़ा⁸ बदलते रहना है
कोई मुझको मिटा नहीं सकता
जश्ने-आदम मना नहीं सकता

---

6. मानव-उत्सव, 7. संप्रदाय, 8. स्वर।

64

Windswept, I have still called the *azaan*
Blown the conchshell in ink-black nights
Hung the cross outside for all to see
I have sought to remove it from every home
Taken it to throw far away from town.

And declared, Awake!
Remove this layer of ice over your heart
Thaw it with the heat of your embrace
Do whatever wrong that you wish to do
But tonight let us celebrate the festival of man.

And yet, it re-emerged from my sleeve
Quickly it just smothered the rekindled flame
Rubbed the darkness on my face again
What the heart wished to say remained unsaid
Having reached the doorstep the *baraat* went away.

Then, calling me aside, it said:
Life today has a name—fear
Fear is that ground on which
Communalism grows, differences sprout
And waves leave the ocean to make their own way.

So long as fear lurks in one's heart
All I need to do is change my face
Change my idiom, the tone of my speech
None can then destroy me
Or celebrate the festival of man.

नेहरू

मैंने तनहा¹ कभी उसको देखा नहीं
फिर भी जब उसको देखा वो तनहा मिला
जैसे सहरा² में चशमा³ कहीं
या समंदर में मीनारे-नूर⁴
या कोई फ़िक्र⁵ औहाम⁶ में
फ़िक्र सदियों अकेली-अकेली रही
ज़ेहन सदियों अकेला-अकेला मिला

और अकेला-अकेला भटकता रहा
हर नये हर पुराने ज़माने में वो
बे-ज़बाँ तीरगी⁷ में कभी
और कभी चीख़ती धूप में
चाँदनी में कभी ख़ाब की
उसकी तक़दीर थी इक मुसलसल⁸ तलाश
ख़ुद को ढूँढा किया हर फ़साने⁹ में वो

बोझ से अपने उसकी कमर झुक गयी
क़द मगर और कुछ और बढ़ता रहा
ख़ैरो-शर¹⁰ की कोई जंग हो
ज़िंदगी का हो कोई जिहाद¹¹
वो हमेशा हुआ सब से पहले शहीद
सबसे पहले वो सूली पे चढ़ता रहा

---

1. अकेली. 2. रेगिस्तान. 3. सोता झरना. 4. प्रकाश स्तम्भ. 5. विचार. 6. अंधविश्वास,
भ्रम (वहम का बहुवचन). 7. अँधेरा. 8. लगातार. 9. कहानी. 10. कल्याण और
उत्पात. 11. युद्ध।

Nehru

Alone, I never saw him
And yet, whenever I saw him he was alone
Like a spring somewhere in the desert
Or a lighthouse in the ocean
Or like thought amidst engulfing prejudice
For centuries, thought has always stood alone
For centuries, consciousness has always stood alone.

And alone he wandered
Through worlds new and old
In mute darkness sometimes
And sometimes in the scorching sun
And sometimes, in the moonlight of a dream
His destiny was an unending search
He looked for himself in every story he read.

Burdens bent his back
But in stature he grew taller still.
In the struggle between good and evil
Or in battles worthy in life
He was always the first martyr
The first always to ascend the cross.

जिन तक़ाज़ों[12] ने उसको दिया था जनम
उनकी आग़ोश[13] में फिर समया न वो
ख़ून में वेद गूँजे हुए
और जबीं[14] पर फ़रोज़ाँ[15] अज़ाँ[16]
और सीने पर रक़्साँ[17] सलीब[18]
बे-झिझक सब के क़ाबू में आता गया
और किसी के भी क़ाबू में आया न वो

हाथ में उसके क्या था जो देता हमें
सिर्फ़ इक कील, उसी कील का इक निशाँ
नशा-ए-मय[19] कोई चीज़ है
इक घड़ी दो घड़ी, एक रात
और हासिल वही दर्दे-सर
उसने ज़िंदाँ[20] में लेकिन पिया था जो ज़हर
उठ के सीने से बैठा न उसका धुआँ

---

12. माँगों, 13. गोद, 14. माथा, 15. दीप्त, आलोकित, 16. नमाज़ का बुलावा, 17.
नाचती हुई, 18. सूली, 19. शराब का नशा, 20. कारागार।

The destiny that gave birth to him
To its fold he never returned.
His blood was seeped in the Vedas
On his forehead glowed the *azaan*
The crucifix dangled across his chest
Willingly he came within the power of all
But never came under the power of any.

What did he have to give to us?
Only a nail, with but one aim.
The inebriation of alcohol, what is it?
It lasts for a moment, or maybe the night
And leaves in return an ache in the head
But the poison he drank in the prison of life
Caused a smoke to arise from his heart that never left.

ग़ज़ल

शोर यूँ ही न परिन्दों[1] ने मचाया होगा,
कोई जंगल की तरफ़ शहर से आया होगा।

पेड़ के काटने वालों को ये मालूम तो था,
जिस्म जल जायेंगे जब सर पे न साया होगा।

बानी-ए-जश्ने बहाराँ[2] ने ये सोचा भी नहीं,
किस ने काँटों को लहू अपना पिलाया होगा।

अपने जंगल से जो घबरा के उड़े थे प्यासे,
ये सराब[3] उन को समंदर नज़र आया होगा।

बिजली के तार पे बैठा हुआ तन्हा पंछी
सोचता है कि वो जंगल तो पराया होगा।

---

1. पक्षियों 2. बंसत उत्सव के प्रेरणा श्रोतों. 3. धोखा।

Ghazal

The birds could not have screeched without a cause
From the town to the jungle someone must have come.

Those who cut the tree could not have but known
The body will burn when the shade is gone.

Intoxicated by spring they never gave a thought
To those who offered their blood to a thorn.

Those who left their jungle anxious and thirsty
Were fooled by the mirage of an ocean perhaps.

Perched on an electric line a lone bird thinks
Not mine was that jungle at all.

देखी ज़माने की यारी

देखी ज़माने की यारी, बिछुड़े सभी बारी-बारी

क्या लेके मिलें अब दुनिया से
आंसू के सिवा कुछ पास नहीं
या फूल ही फूल थे, दामन में
या कांटों को भी आस नहीं

मतलब की दुनिया है सारी, बिछुड़े सभी बारी-बारी

वक़्त है मेहरबाँ, आरज़ू है जवाँ
फ़िक्र कल की करें, इतनी फ़ुरसत कहाँ

दौर यह चलता, रहे
रूप मचलता रहे
रंग उछलता रहे
जाम बदलता रहे

रात भर मेहमाँ हैं बहारे यहाँ
रात जब ढल गयी फिर ये खुशियाँ कहाँ

बढ़ने लगी बेक़रारी, बिछुड़े सभी बारी-बारी

Enough! The Loyalty of Friends

Enough! The loyalty of friends I too have seen
One by one they left till none was on the scene.

With what can I seek to meet with the rest
I have only with me tears at best
Once flowers, only flowers, were my life's concern
Now, for even a thorn I do not yearn.

Enongh! This world is full of the selfish and the mean
One by one they left till none was on the scene.

The tide is on your side, and desire still aflame
Who has the time to think then of the morrow's claim?

Let the moment ride
And forms collide
Let colours dance
And wine entrance.

But alas! The tide is yours only for the night
And when the night wanes, 'tis happiness' blight!

Enough! Anxiety grows, in patterns unseen
One by one they left till none was on the scene.

उड़ जा, उड़ जा, प्यासे भँवरे
रस न मिलेगा ख़ारों में
काग़ज़ के फूल यहाँ खिलते हों
बैठ न उन गुलज़ारों में
नादान तमन्ना रेती में
उम्मीद की किश्ती खेती है
इक हाथ से देती है दुनिया
सौ हाथों से ले लेती है

यह खेल है कब से जारी, बिछुड़े सभी बारी-बारी

(फ़िल्म *काग़ज़ के फूल* से)

Fly away! Fly away, O thirsty moth
No nectar will flow from these thorns
Where bloom only paper flowers
'Tis no use to be lovelorn.
Desire, innocent, seeks to row
The boat of hope through sand
One hand may give, but to take away here
Hundreds are at hand.

Enough! This play too often I have seen,
One by one they left till none was on the scene.

(From the film *Kaagaz ke Phool*)

ग़ज़ल

वो भी सराहने लगे अरबाबे-फ़न[1] के बाद
दादे-सुख़न[2] मिली मुझे तर्के-वतन[3] के बाद

दीवानावार चाँद से आगे निकल गये
ठहरा न दिल कहीं भी तेरी अंजुमन के बाद

एलाने-हक़ में ख़तरा-ए-दारो-रसन[4] तो है
लेकिन सवाल ये है कि दारो-रसन के बाद

होंटों को सी के देखिए पछताइये गा आप
हंगामे जाग उठते हैं अकसर घुटन के बाद

गुरबत[5] की ठंडी छाँव में याद आयी है उसकी धूप
क़द्रे-वतन[6] हुई हमें तर्के-वतन के बाद

इंसाँ की ख़्वाहिशों की कोई इंतेहा नहीं
दो गज़ ज़मीन चाहिए, दो गज़ कफ़न के बाद

---

1. कलाकारगण, 2. कविता की प्रशंसा, 3. वतन छोड़ना, 4. फाँसी पाने का खतरा,
5. परदेश, 6. वतन के मूल्य की पहचान।

Ghazal

Once the masters had praised, they too were not hostile,
My poetry won respect, when I became an exile.

I searched far beyond the heedless moon's boundary,
The heart found no solace, without your company.

In proclaiming the truth hangs the fear of the gallows,
But the question is, after that what follows?

Seal your lips and see, you will regret the act,
If a lull is enforced, the storm will attack.

In the shadows of exile, we think of the motherland's sun,
Until I was abroad the homeland remained unsung.

There are no limits to a man's endless wants,
Beyond two yards of shroud, two yards of land too he demands.

वक़्त ने किया

वक़्त ने किया क्या हंसी सितम
तुम रहे न तुम, हम रहे न हम

बेक़रार दिल इस तरह मिले
जिस तरह कभी हम जुदा न थे
तुम भी खो गये, हम भी खो गये
एक राह पे चलके दो क़दम

जायेंगे कहाँ, सूझता नहीं
चल पड़ें मगर रास्ता नहीं
क्या तलाश है कुछ पता नहीं
बुन रहे हैं दिल ख़्वाब दम-ब-दम[1]

वक़्त ने किया क्या हसीं सितम
तुम रहे न तुम, हम रहे न हम

(फिल्म काग़ज़ के फूल से)

---

1. प्रति पल।

With Such Sweet Revenge

With such sweet revenge time cast its die
You remained not you, I remained not I.

Anxious hearts met in such a way
As if we never had gone astray,
You soon were lost, lost too was I
But two steps together on one pathway.

Where can we go, no answer can we find
We could begin to walk, no avenue would we find,
What is it we seek, we don't have a clue
Our hearts weave a dream, each moment, 'tis true.

With such sweet revenge time cast its die
You remained not you, I remained not I.

(From the film *Kaagaz ke Phool*)

तज़दीद

तलातुम,[1] वलवले,[2] हैजान,[3] अरमान
सब उसके साथ रुख़्सत हो चुके थे
यक़ीं था अब न हँसना है न रोना
कुछ इतना हँस चुके थे रो चुके थे

किसी ने आज इक अँगड़ाई लेकर
नज़र में रेशमी गिरहें लगा दीं
तलातुम, वलवले, हैजान, अरमान
वहीं चिंगारियाँ फिर मुस्करा दीं

---

1. बाढ़, तूफ़ान, उद्वेग, 2. उमंगे, 3. उद्विग्नता।

Renewal

Tumults, desires, storms and hopes
Left when she said goodbye
I believed that I could neither laugh nor cry
I had already laughed and cried so much.

Yet, today, someone stretching her limbs
Threw rings of silk around my eyes
Tumults, desires, storms and hopes
The very sparks ignited once again.

ग़ज़ल

ख़ारो-ख़स[1] तो उठें, रास्ता तो चले
मैं अगर थक गया, क़ाफ़िला तो चले

चाँद-सूरज बुज़ुर्गो के नक़्शे-क़दम[2]
ख़ैर बुझने दो इनको, हवा तो चले

हाकिमे-शहर, ये भी कोई शहर है
मस्ज़िदें बंद हैं, मयकदा[3] तो चले

इसको मज़हब कहो या सियासत[4] कहो
ख़ुदकुशी का हुनर तुम सिखा तो चले

इतनी लाशें में कैसे उठा पाऊँगा
आप ईंटों की हुरमत[5] बचा तो चले

बेलचे लाओ, खोलो ज़मीं की तहें
मैं कहाँ दफ़्न हूँ, कुछ पता तो चले

---

1. काँटे और तिनके, घास-फूस, झाड़-झंखाड़. 2. पद-चिह. 3. लय. 4. राजनीति.
5. मर्यादा।

Ghazal

The weeds may flourish, let the path go on
Even if I am tired, let the caravan move on.

The sun and moon—our ancestors' guides
Even if they extinguish, let the breeze move on.

O, rulers of the town, what sort of town is this?
The mosques may be closed, let the taverns run on.

Call it faith, or the craft of politics
The art of suicide you taught us well.

So many corpses, how will I shoulder them?
The virtue of bricks you preserved so well.

Bring the shovels, open earth's layers
Where I am buried, let me know as well.

आदत

मुद्दतों मैं इक अंधे कुएँ में असीर[1]
सर पटकता रहा, गिड़गिड़ाता रहा
रौशनी चाहिये, चाँदनी चाहिये, ज़िंदगी चाहिये
रौशनी प्यार की, चाँदनी यार की, ज़िंदगी दार[2] की

अपनी आवाज़ सुनता रहा रात-दिन
धीरे-धीरे यक़ीं दिल को आता रहा
सूने संसार में
बे-वफ़ा यार में
दामने-दार[3] में
रौशनी भी नहीं
चाँदनी भी नहीं
ज़िंदगी भी नहीं
ज़िंदगी एक रात
वाहमा[4] कायनात[5]
आदमी बे-सबात[6]
लोग कोताह क़द
शहर, शहरे-हसद[7]
गाँव इनसे भी बद।
इन अँधेरों ने जब पीस डाला मुझे
फिर अचानक कुएँ ने उछाला मुझे
अपने सीने से बाहर निकाला मुझे

---

1. बंदी, 2. फाँसी, 3. फाँसी का गोद, 4. भ्रम, 5. सृष्टि, 6. नश्वर, क्षणभंगुर, 7. ईर्ष्या
के नगर।

Habit

For aeons, I was imprisoned in a blind well
I kept beating my head, kept muttering to myself:
I want the sunlight, I want the moonlight, I want life itself
The sunlight of love, the moonlight of friends, the freedom of
death.

Day and night I heard only my voice
And gradually I came to believe
In this lonesome world
In the disloyalty of friends
In the lap of the gallows
There is no sunlight
There is no moonlight
There is no life,
Life is one long night
The world an illusion
Man transient
People dwarfed
Towns, citadels of envy
Villages even worse.
When this darkness had completely crushed me
The well, suddenly, ejected me
From its depths it expelled me.

सैकड़ों मिन्न थे सामने
सैकड़ों उसके बाज़ार थे
एक बूढ़ी जुलेख़ा नहीं
जाने कितने ख़रीदार थे
बढ़ता जाता था यूसुफ़ का मोल
लोग बिकने को तैयार थे
खुल गये महजबीनों⁸ के सर
रेशमी चादरें हट गयीं
पलकें झपकीं न नज़रें झुकीं
मरमरी⁹ उँगलियाँ कट गयीं
हाथ दामन तक आया कोई
धज्जियाँ दूर तक बट गयीं

मैंने डर के लगा दी कुएँ में छलांग
सर पटकने लगा फिर उसी कर्ब¹⁰ से
फिर उसी दर्द से गिड़गिड़ाने लगा
रौशनी चाहिये, चाँदनी चाहिये, ज़िंदगी चाहिये

---

8. चंद्रमुखी जिसका माथा चाँद जैसा उज्ज्वल हो, 9. संगमरमर जैसी श्वेत, गोरी, 10.
पीड़ा।

I saw before me a million Egyptians
There were a million bazaars
Not one aged Zulekha there was
God knows how many buyers there were
Yusuf's price constantly rose
And people were willing to be sold.
Suddenly, everyone's luminous faces were unveiled
Their silken sheets were cast away
No eyes blinked, no glance was lowered
Fingers, marble-white, were cut aside
If a hand came close to a garment
The body was dismembered, scattered wide.

Afraid, I jumped back into the well
Began to beat my head with the same agony
I began to grovel again with the same pleading:
I want the sunlight, I want the moonlight, I want life itself.

दावत

कोई देता है दरे-दिल पे मुसलसल आवाज़
और फिर अपनी ही आवाज़ से घबराता है
अपने बदले हुए अंदाज़ का एहसास नहीं
मेरे बहके हुए अंदाज़ से घबराता है
साज़ उठाया है कि मौसम का तक़ाज़ा था यही
काँपता हाथ मगर साज़ से घबराता है
राज़ को है किसी हमराज़ की मुद्दत से तलाश
और दिल सुहबते-हमराज़ से घबराता है
शौक़ ये है कि उड़े वो तो ज़मीं साथ उड़े
हौसला ये है कि परवाज़[1] से घबराता है
तेरी तक़दीर में आसाइशे-अंजाम[2] नहीं
ऐ कि तू शोरिशे-आग़ाज़[3] से घबराता है

कभी आगे, कभी पीछे कोई रफ़्तार है ये
हमको रफ़्तार का आहंग[4] बदलना होगा
ज़ेहन के वास्ते साँचे तो न ढालेगी हयात
ज़ेहन को आप ही हर साँचे में ढलना होगा
ये भी जलना कोई जलना है कि शोला न धुआँ
अब जला देंगे ज़माने को जो जलना होगा
रास्ते घूम के सब जाते हैं मंज़िल की तरफ़
हम किसी रुख़ से चलें, साथ ही चलना होगा

---

1. उड़ान, 2. परिणति का सुख, 3. आरम्भ का कोलाहल, 4. लय, सामंजस्य।

Invitation

Someone calls out to my heart ceaselessly
And then is, of his own voice, nervous
Unaware of how his mien has changed
My mien of abandon makes him nervous.
The lute was the call of the season
But to play on it our hands were nervous.
For ages a secret has searched a confidant
But the confidant's demeanour makes us nervous.
You want the earth to soar with you
But your resolve is such, that to take wing you are nervous.
Your destiny will lack peace and fulfilment
The clamour of beginnings makes you nervous.

Sometimes forward and sometimes backwards—is this any

pace?

The rhythm of our movement, we'll have to change.
Life will not mould vessels for our thoughts
Our thoughts must learn to fit each receptacle.
Is this a way to burn, no ember no smoke?
The world must burn to see a burning spectacle.
All roads lead to but one destination
Wherever we begin, unity must be our vehicle.

चराग़ां

एक-दो भी नहीं छब्बीस दिये
एक-इक करके जलाये मैंने

इक दिया नाम का आज़ादी के
उसने जलते हुए होंटों से कहा
चाहे जिस मुल्क से गेहूँ माँगो
हाथ फैलाने की आज़ादी है

इक दिया नाम का खुशहाली के
उसके जलते ही यह मालूम हुआ
कितनी बदहाली है
पेट ख़ाली है मेरा, जेब मेरी ख़ाली है

इक दिया नाम का यकजहती[1] के
रौशनी उसकी जहाँ तक पहुँची
कौम को लड़ते-झगड़ते देखा
माँ के आंचल में हैं जितने पैवंद
सबको इक साथ उधड़ते देखा

दूर से बीवी ने झल्ला के कहा
तेल महँगा भी है, मिलता भी नहीं
क्यों दिये इतने जला रक्खे हैं
अपने घर में न झरोखा न मुँडेर
ताक़ सपनों के सजा रक्खे हैं

---

1. एकता

90

Lamps

Not one, but twenty-six lamps,
One by one, I have lighted today.

One I lit in the name of freedom
With burning lips it said:
Ask for wheat from any nation
We have the freedom to beg.

One I lit in the name of prosperity
The moment it was lighted
It illuminated our confused reality:
My stomach is empty, my pocket is empty.

One I lit in the name of unity
Wherever its light was able to reach
We saw communities lose amity
We saw a mother's shelter breach
Its joints coming apart simultaneously.

Exasperated, my wife shouted out
Oil is dear and just not there
Why have you lighted so many lamps
No balcony or terrace, our house is bare
There is no place for dreams anywhere.

आया गुस्से का एक ऐसा झोंका
बुझ गये सारे दिये
हाँ मगर एक दिया नाम है जिसका उमीद
झिलमिलाता ही चला जाता है!

A wave of anger
Blew away the lamps
But, yes, just one remained,
Its name is hope, and it flickers on.

जाने क्या ढूँढती रहती हैं

जाने क्या ढूंढती रहती हैं ये आँखें मुझमें
राख के ढेर में शोला है न चिंगारी है

अब न वह प्यार, न उस प्यार की यादें बाक़ी
आग यूं दिल में लगी, कुछ न रहा, कुछ न बचा
जिसकी तस्वीर निगाहों में लिये बैठी हो
मैं वह दिलदार, नहीं उसकी हूँ ख़ामोश चिता
जाने क्या ढूँढती रहती हैं

ज़िंदगी हँसके गुज़रती तो बहुत अच्छा था,
ख़ैर, हँसके न सही, रोके गुज़र जायेगी
राख बरबाद मुहब्बत की बचा रखी है
बार-बार इसकी जो छेड़ा तो बिखर जायेगी
जाने क्या ढूँढती रहती हैं

आरज़ू जुर्म, वफ़ा[1] जुर्म, तमन्ना है गुनाह
यह वह दुनिया है जहाँ प्यार नहीं हो सकता
कैसे बाज़ार का दस्तूर तुझे समझाऊँ
बिक गया जो वह ख़रीदार नहीं हो सकता

(फिल्म *शोला और शबनम* से)

---

1. निष्ठा।

94

I Do Not Know What These Eyes

I do not know what these eyes seek from me
In this heap of ash, there is neither spark nor ember.

Now, there's no longer that love, or even its memory
Nothing was left, nothing remained, when the heart was
                                              ravaged by fire,
The image that you still nurture in your eyes
I am not that vibrant person, only his extinguished pyre.
I do not know what these eyes seek from me.

Laughter could well have been life's companion
If not, life will still pass by tearfully,
The ashes of our ruined love are still preserved by me
They will disperse if you touch them repeatedly.
I do not know what these eyes seek from me.

Desire is crime, loyalty vice, want a sin
This is a world where love is not possible,
How do I explain to you the custom of the market
One who is bought cannot be a buyer.

(From the film *Shola aur Shabnam*)

आवारा सज्दे

(कम्युनिस्ट इकाई के टूटने पर)

इक यही सोज़े-निहाँ[1] कुल मेरा सरमाया[2] है
दोस्तो, मैं किसे ये सोज़े-निहाँ नज़्र[3] करूँ
कोई क़ातिल सरे-मक़्तल[4] नज़र आता ही नहीं
किस को दिल नज़्र करूँ और किसे जाँ नज़्र करूँ

तुम भी महबूब मेरे, तुम भी हो दिलदार[5] मेरे
आशना[6] मुझसे मगर तुम भी नहीं, तुम भी नहीं
ख़त्म है तुम पे मसीहानफ़सी,[7] चारागरी[8]
महरमे-दर्दे-जिगर,[9] तुम भी नहीं, तुम भी नहीं

अपनी लाश आप उठाना कोई आसान नहीं
दस्तो-बाज़ू[10] मेरे नाकारा हुए जाते हैं
जिनसे हर दौर में चमकी है तुम्हारी दहलीज़
आज सज्दे वही आवारा हुए जाते हैं

दूर मंज़िल थी, मगर ऐसी भी कुछ दूर न थी
लेके फिरती रही रस्ते ही में वहशत[11] मुझको
एक ज़ख़्म ऐसा न खाया कि बहार आ जाती
दार[12] तक ले के गया शौक़े-शहादत मुझको

राह में टूट गये पाँव तो मालूम हुआ
जुज़[13] मेरे और मेरा रहनुमा[14] कोई नहीं
एक के बाद ख़ुदा एक चला आता था
कह दिया अक़्ल ने तंग आके ख़ुदा कोई नहीं

---

1. छुपी हुई तपिश या पीड़ा. 2. पूँजी. 3. भेंट. 4. वध-स्थल पर. 5. प्रिय. 6. परिचित.
7. ईसा मसीह की साँस का गुण, जो मुर्दे जिला देता था. 8. उपचार इलाज. 9. जिगर
का दर्द जानने वाला. 10. हाथ और भुजाएँ. 11. उन्माद. 12. फाँसी. सूली.
13. अलावा. 14 मार्गदर्शक।

Vagrant Worship
(When the Communist Party split)

This internal anguish is all the wealth I have
Friends, whom should I bequeath this anguish to?
No murderer can be seen at the spot of the crime
This heart, this life, whom should I bequeath to?
You are my beloved, and you my adored
And yet, known to me, is neither of you.
You are the reviver of the dead, you are the cure
And yet, my pain's healer, is neither of you.
It is not easy to lift one's own corpse
My arms falter, they begin to fail me.
It is true their obeisance brightened your threshold
But today, those salutations lack loyalty.
The goal was far, and yet not that far
For me to lose all sense of bearing.
I could not give my blood to bring the colour of spring
Although the desire for martyrdom took me often towards the
                                                         gallows
I realized then when my feet gave way
That this journey has no other guide but me.
One after the other, saviours kept coming
Until, fed up, the intellect said, there is no divinity.

आख़िरी रात

चाँद टूटा पिघल गये तारे
क़तरा-क़तरा टपक रही है रात
पलकें आँखों पे झुकती आती हैं
अंखड़ियों में खटक रही है रात
आज छेड़ो न कोई अफ़साना
आज की रात हमको सोने दो

खुलते जाते हैं सिमटे सिकुड़े जाल
घुलते जाते हैं ख़ून में बादल
अपने गुलनार' पंख फैलाये
आ रहे है इसी तरफ़ जंगल
गुल करो शम्अ, रख दो पैमाना
आज की रात हमको सोने दो

शाम से पहले मर चुका था शहर
कौन दरवाज़ा खटखटाता है
और ऊँची करो ये दीवारें
शोर आँगन में आया जाता है
कह दो है आज बंद मयख़ाना
आज की रात हमको सोने दो

जिस्म ही जिस्म हैं, कफ़न ही कफ़न
बात सुनते न सर झुकाते हैं

---

1. अनार के फूल के रंग का।

The Last Night

The moon has broken, the stars have melted
The night is measured in drops,
Eyelids droop to kiss the eyes
In the eyes remains the night,
Tonight tell me no tales, I beg
Tonight let me sleep, I beg.

Webs, stiff and tight, begin to unwind
Clouds begin to dissolve in my blood,
Their ruby-coloured wings outstretched
The jungles are advancing this way,
Extinguish the flame, put the goblet down
Tonight let me sleep, I beg.

Before dusk the town had died
Who now knocks at the door?
Raise the walls higher still
The noise of the street is filtering in,
Announce that today the tavern is closed
Tonight let me sleep, I beg.

Only bodies exist, only shrouds
They can neither hear nor nod their heads,

अम्न की ख़ैर, कोतवाल की ख़ैर
मुर्दे क़ब्रों से निकले आते हैं
कोई अपना न कोई बेगाना²
आज की रात हमको सोने दो

कोई कहता था, ठीक कहता था
सरकशी³ बन गयी है सबका शआर⁴
क़त्ल पर जिनको एतराज़ न था
दफ़्न होने को क्यों नहीं तैयार
होशमंदी⁵ है आज सो जाना
आज की रात हमको सोने दो

---

2. पराया, 3. विद्रोह, 4. आदत, स्वभाव, 5. सजगता, समझदारी।

May peace flourish and the Kotwal prosper
Corpses come out from their graves,
None is a friend, and no one a stranger
Tonight let me sleep, I beg.

Someone used to say, and rightly so,
It has become the habit of all to protest,
Those who took a murder in their stride
Why do they so much a burial detest?
Wisdom it is to sleep today
Tonight let me sleep, I beg.

कोई ये कैसे बताए

कोई ये कैसे बताए के वो तन्हा क्यों है
वो जो अपना था वही और किसी का क्यों है
यही दुनिया है तो फिर ऐसी ये दुनिया क्यों है
यही होता है तो आख़िर यही होता क्यों है

तुम मस्सरत का कहो या इसे ग़म का रिश्ता
कहते हैं प्यार का रिश्ता है जनम का रिश्ता
है जनम का जो ये रिश्ता तो बदलता क्यों है

इक ज़रा हाथ बढ़ा ले तो पकड़ ले दामन
उनके सीने में समा जाए हमारी धड़कन
इतनी क़ुरबत है तो फिर फ़ासला इतना क्यों है

दिले बरबाद से निकला नहीं अब तक कोई
एक लुटे घर पे दिया करता है दस्तक कोई
आस जो टूट गई फिर से बँधाता क्यों है

(फ़िल्म अर्थ से)

102

How Does One Explain

How does one explain why he is so lonely?
Why is the one who was mine, not mine only?
If this is how the world is, then why is it so?
If this is what happens, why does it happen so?

Call it a bond of joy or that of sorrow
They say that the bond of love is eternal
If that is so, why does it change so often?

If you stretch out a hand, I'll reach out and hold you
Place my heartbeat forever in your heart
If there's so much closeness between us, why do we stand so
                                                    far apart?

No one has ever escaped the heart's desolation
When someone knocks on a ravaged house
Why does it resurrect a hope that has broken?

(From the film *Arth*)

कर चले हम फ़िदा

कर चले हम फ़िदा[1] जानो-तन, साथियो
अब तुम्हारे हवाले वतन, साथियो
साँस थमती गयी, नब्ज़ जमती गयी
फिर भी बढ़ते क़दम को न रुकने दिया
कट गये सर हमारे तो कुछ ग़म नहीं
सर हिमालय का हमने न झुकने दिया
   मरते-मरते रहा बांकपन, साथियो
      अब तुम्हारे हवाले वतन, साथियो
ज़िन्दा रहने के मौसम बहुत हैं मगर
जान देने की रुत रोज़ आती नहीं
हुस्न और इश्क़ दोनों को रुस्वा करे
वह जवानी जो ख़ूँ में नहाती नहीं
      आज धरती बनी है दुल्हन, साथियो
      अब तुम्हारे हवाले वतन, साथियो
राह क़ुर्बानियों की न वीरान हो
तुम सजाते ही रहना नये क़ाफ़िले
फ़त्ह का जश्न इस जश्न के बाद है
ज़िन्दगी मौत से मिल रही है गले
      बाँध लो अपने सर से कफ़न, साथियो
      अब तुम्हारे हवाले वतन, साथियो
खींच दो अपने ख़ूँ से ज़मीं पर लकीर
इस तरफ़ आने पाये न रावन कोई
तोड़ दो हाथ अगर हाथ उठने लगे
छूने पाये न सीता का दामन कोई
      राम भी तुम, तुम्हीं लक्ष्मण, साथियो
      अब तुम्हारे हवाले वतन, साथियो

(फिल्म हक़ीक़त से)

---

1. निछावर।

We Have Given Our Lives

We have given our lives, comrades
Now we leave the country in your hands, comrades
The breath gave way, the pulse fell feeble
Yet nothing could stop our marching ahead
Our heads were cut, it didn't matter much
We kept high the Himalayas' head.
We were full of abandon as we died, comrades
Now in your hands we leave the country, comrades.
The seasons to live are many, but
The season to die comes just once
Beauty and love are both not valued
By youth yet unfamiliar with blood.
Today, the earth is a bride, comrades
Now in your hands we leave the country, comrades.
May the path of sacrifice never be solitary
May the number of caravans increase
This celebration now, before that of victory
Life right now is embracing death.
Tie shrouds on your heads, comrades
Now in your hands we leave the country, comrades
With your blood draw a line on the ground
Let no Ravana cross it ever
Smash the hand if hands are raised
Let no one ever touch the garment of Sita.
You are Rama, you are Laxman too, comrades
Now in your hands we leave the country, comrades.

(From the film *Haqeeqat*)

धमाका

(चारु मजुमदार की याद में)

कोई चौराहा हो चाहे कोई नाका, दोस्तो!
हर घड़ी हर दम कोई ताज़ा धमाका, दोस्तो!
यह धमाका बस धमाका है,
धमाके के सिवा कुछ भी नहीं
रोटी दे सकता नहीं
यह रोज़ी दे सकता नहीं
यह कुछ भी दे सकता नहीं
इसकी जेबों में न दुनिया है न दीन[1]
इसकी मुठ्ठी में न ज़र[2] है न ज़मीन
रूस है इसकी निगाहों में न चीन
यह धमाका बस धमाका है, धमाके के सिवा कुछ भी नहीं
मैं खड़ा था कबसे इस ख़ामोश क़ब्रिस्तान में
क़ब्रें सब ख़मोश थीं
क़ब्रों में रहने वाले सब ख़ामोश थे
खा रहे थे कीड़े चुपके-चुपके बोसीदा[3] कफ़न
सब्ज़, नीले, पीली सेह-रंगे[4] कफ़न
लाशें सब नंगी थीं लाशों के सिवा[5] नंगे कफ़न
मैंने हाथों को हिलाया इस तरह
कोने-कोने में धमाका हो गया

---

1. धर्म, 2. सोना, धन, 3. सड़ा-गला, 4. तिरंगे, 5. अधिक।

Explosion

(In memory of Charu Mazumdar)

At a crossing it may be, or at any other place, my friends!
At each moment a new explosion, my friends!
This explosion is just an explosion,
Nothing but an explosion.
It cannot provide bread
Or employment
Or anything else.
In its pocket is neither the world nor God
In its grasp is neither gold nor land
It eyes are not on Russia or China
This explosion is just an explosion, nothing but an explosion.
I was standing for so long in this silent cemetery
The graves were silent
Their inhabitants silent
Maggots were silently eating the rotting coffins
Green, blue, yellow, multi-coloured coffins
The corpses were naked, the coffins more so
I just moved my hands
And there was an explosion

ये धमाका बस धमाका है, धमाके के सिवा कुछ भी नहीं
वो भी तो बस इक धमाका था धमाके के सिवा कुछ भी न था
जिससे उछलीं कहकशाएँ[6]
जिससे उभरी कायनात[7]
घर से जब भी निकलो बाहर, दोस्तो!
कुछ धमाके भर लो अपनी जेब में

हर घड़ी हर दम कोई ताज़ा धमाका दोस्तो!
कौन जाने कोई ज़र्रा[8] टूट जाय

---

6. आकाशगंगाएँ, 7. सृष्टि, 8. कण।

This explosion is just an explosion, nothing but an explosion.
That too was just an explosion, nothing but an explosion
Which brought forth galaxies
And brought forth creation.
Whenever you leave your homes, friends,
Fill your pockets with a few explosions.

At each moment a new explosion, my friends!
Who knows, an atom may split.

तबस्सुम

इक कली नूरदीदए-गुलज़ार[1]
गौहरे-शब[2] चिरागे-बाग़ो-बहार[3]
नर्म, नाज़ुक शगुफ़्ता, लालगूँ
शोख़, मासूम बे-जुबाँ, तर्रार[4]
मुझ पे रंगीनियाँ लुटाती थी

लुत्फ़े नज़्ज़ारगी[5] मिटा ही दिया
मैंने दस्ते-तलब[6] बढ़ा ही दिया
पंखड़ी में निहाँ थी चिनगारी
हाथ जिसने मेरा जला ही दिया
और कली मुझ पे मुस्कराती थी

---

1. उपवन की आँखों की ज्योति (बेटी), 2. रात का मोती, 3. प्रकाशमान दीप,
4. चंचल, 5. सुन्दर दृश्य देखने का आनन्द, 6. कामना का हाथ।

Smile

This bud—garden's progeny, scattering light
The glow of spring, pearl of the night
Tender, delicate, unopened, flashy
Mischievous, innocent, mute, saucy
Once showered enticements on me.

But, alas, I destroyed the joy of the sight
I extended the hand of desire inevitably
Within the bud was a spark waiting to ignite
A spark that burnt my hand completely
And the bud kept smiling at me.

नज़राना[1]

तुम परेशान न हो, बाबे-करम[2]-वा[3] न करो
और कुछ देर पुकारूँगा चला जाऊँगा
इसी कूचे में जहाँ चाँद उगा करते हैं
शबे-तारीक[4] गुज़ारूँगा, चला जाऊँगा

रास्ता भूल गया या यही मंज़िल है मेरी
कोई लाया है कि खुद आया हूँ मालूम नहीं
कहते हैं हुस्न की नज़रे भी हंसीं होती हैं
मैं भी कुछ लाया हूँ, क्या लाया हूँ मालूम नहीं

यूँ तो जो कुछ था मेरे पास मैं सब बेच आया
कहीं इनाम मिला, और कहीं क़ीमत भी नहीं
कुछ तुम्हारे लिए आँखों में छुपा रक्खा है
देख लो और न देखो तो शिकायत भी नहीं

एक तो इतनी हसीं दूसरे ये आराइश[5]
जो नज़र पड़ती है चैहरे पे ठहर जाती है
मुस्करा देती हो रस्मन[6] भी अगर महफ़िल में
इक धनक टूट के सीनों में बिखर जाती है

---

1. उपहार, भेंट, 2. कृपा-द्वार, 3. खोलना, 4. अँधेरी रात, 5. सजावट, 6. औपचारिकता रूप से,

A Humble Gift

Don't worry, don't open the doors of kindness
I will call out for a while, then go away,
In this very lane where the moon once bloomed
I will spend a dark night, and go away.

Have I lost the way, or is this my destination?
Has someone brought me here, or have I come on my own?
The gaze of beauty, they say, is beautiful too
I too have brought something, what, I do not know.

Whatever I possessed I sold it off
Sometimes I was rewarded, sometimes I got nothing at all,
Something I have still kept hidden for you in my eyes
If you can see it, and even if you can't, I have no complaints at
all.

You are so beautiful, and then this adornment
Any gaze that falls on you gets arrested on your face
It you smile even out of courtesy
It's as though a rainbow split and spread in the heart.

गर्म बोसों[7] से तराशा हुआ नाज़ुक पैकर[8]
जिसकी इक आँच से हर रूह पिघल जाती है
मैंने सोचा है तो सब सोचते होंगे शायद
प्यास इस तरह भी क्या साँचे में ढल जाती है

क्या कमी है जो करोगी मेरा नज़राना क़बूल
चाहने वाले बहुत, चाह के अफ़साने बहुत
एक ही रात सही गर्मी-ए-हंगाम-ए इश्क़[9]
एक ही रात में जल मरते हैं परवाने बहुत

फिर भी इक रात में सौ तरह के मोड़ आते हैं
काश तुमको कभी तनहाई का एहसास न हो
काश ऐसा न हो घेरे रहे दुनिया तुमको
और इस तरह कि जिस तरह कोई पास न हो

आज की रात जो मेरी ही तरह तनहा है
मैं किसी तरह गुज़ारूँगा चला जाऊँगा
तुम परेशान न हो, बाबे-करम वा न करो
और कुछ देर पुकारूँगा चला जाऊँगा

---

7. चुम्बन, 8. शरीर, बदन, 9. इश्के हंगामें की गर्मी।

Passionate kisses have chiselled this delicate body
Whose one flame can melt any soul
If I have thought so, others too must have
Can thirst for somebody become the only goal?

What do you lack that you will accept my gift?
So many admirers, and tales of desire surround you
True, the heat of love lasts but one night
In one night many moths are burnt to death.

Yet, one night can see a hundred twists
May you never know what it is to feel alone
May it not happen that the world surrounds you so
That there is no one whom you can call your own.

This night, which is lonely like me,
Somehow it will pass, and I will go away
Don't worry, don't open the doors of kindness
I will call out for a while then go away.

अजनबी

ऐ हमा-रंग¹, हमा-नूर², हमा-सोज़ो-गदाज़³
बज़्मे-महताब⁴ से आने की ज़रूरत क्या थी
तू जहाँ थी उसी जन्नत में निखरता तेरा रूप
इस जहन्नुम को बसाने की ज़रूरत क्या थी

ये ख़ुदो-ख़ाल⁵ ये ख़ाबों से तराशा हुआ जिस्म
और दिल जिस पे ख़ुदो-ख़ाल की नर्मी भी निसार
ख़ार⁶ ही ख़ार, शरारे⁷ ही शरारे हैं यहाँ
और थम-थम के उठा पाँव बहारों की बहार

तशनगी⁸ ज़हर भी पी जाती है अमृत की तरह
जाने किस जाम पे रुक जाये निगाहे-मासूम
डूबते देखा है जिन आंखों में मैख़ाना भी
प्यास उन आँखों की बुझे या न बुझे क्या मालूम

हैं सभी हुस्न-परस्त⁹ अह्ले-नज़र¹⁰ साहबे-दिल¹¹
कोई घर में, कोई महफ़िल में सजायेगा तुझे
तू फ़क़त जिस्म नहीं, शेर भी है, गीत भी है
कौन अश्कों¹² की घनी छाँव में गायेगा तुझे

तुझसे इक दर्द का रिश्ता भी है बस प्यार नहीं
अपने आँचल पे मुझे अश्क बहा लेने दे
तू जहाँ जाती है जा, रोकने वाला मैं कौन
रस्ते-रस्ते में मगर शम्अ जला लेने दे

---

1. समस्त रंग, 2. समस्त ज्योति, 3. समस्त कोमलता और तपिश 4. चंद्रसभा, 5. गाल और तिल, 6. काँटा, 7. चिंगारी. 8. प्यास, 9. रूप के पुजारी 10. दृष्टि वाले, 11. दिल वाले, 12. आँसू।

Stranger

O, fullness of colour, pervasive light, the burning heart of
                                                desire
Why did you leave the company of the moon?
Where you were, in paradise, your beauty would have only
                                                grown
What was the need to settle down on this hell?

This cheek, its beauty spot, this body chiselled by dreams
A heart so soft, even the cheeks view it with envy
Only thorns abound here, only sparks
O, choicest bloom of spring, pick your way more carefully.

Thirst can swallow poison too as though it were nectar
On which goblet the innocent's eye will fall, who knows?
Eyes in which we have seen taverns drown
Will their thirst be slaked, or not, who knows?

All are worshippers of beauty, connoisseurs, people of heart
Their homes, the gatherings of friends, you will adorn
Not merely flesh, you are poetry, you are song
Who will sing you when dark, tearful clouds form?

I have with you a bond of pain, not of just love
Give me your garment to soak my tears as they flow
Go where you wish, who am I to say don't
But let me light a candle on the path where you go.

इब्ने-मरियम

तुम खुदा हो
खुदा के बेटे हो
या फ़क़त अम्न के पयम्बर हो
या किसी का हसीं तख़य्युल[1] हो
जो भी हो मुझको अच्छे लगते हो
मुझको सच्चे लगते हो

इस सितारे में, जिसमें सदियों के
झूठ और किज़्ब[2] का अँधेरा है
इस सितारे में, जिसको हर रुख़ से
रंगती सरहदों ने घेरा है
इस सितारे में, जिसकी आबादी
अम्न बोती है जंग काटती है
रात पीती है नूर[3] मुखड़ों का
सुब्ह[4] सीनों का ख़ून चाटती है
तुम न होते तो जाने क्या होता

तुम न होते तो इस सितारे में
देवता, राक्षस, गुलाम, इमाम,
पारसा[5], रिंद[6], राहबर[7], रहजन[8]
बरहमन, शैख़, पादरी, भिक्षु
सभी होते मगर हमारे लिए
कौन चढ़ता खुशी से सूली पर

---

1. कल्पना, 2. मक्कारी, 3. ज्योति, चमक, 4. प्रातःकाल, 5. पवित्र आत्मा, 6. शराबी,
7. पथप्रदर्शक, 8. बटमार, लुटेरे।

Ibn-e-Mariam

Are you God?
The son of God?
Or only a messenger of peace?
Or someone's beautiful creation?
Whoever you are, I like you.
You seem like the truth to me.

On this planet, where for centuries
Lies and deceit have prevailed,
On this planet, which from every corner
By crawling boundaries has been tamed,
On this planet, whose people
Sow peace and reap war,
Night sucks the lustre off faces
And the dawn licks the blood off chests,
If you were not here, what would happen?

If you were not here, then on this planet
Gods, demons, slaves, priests,
Innocents, drunks, guides, looters
Pundits, preachers, padres, mendicants
Would all be here, but, for us
Who would have gladly ascended the cross?

झोंपड़ों में घिरा ये वीराना
मछलियाँ दिन में सूखती हैं जहाँ
बिल्लियाँ दूर बैठी रहती हैं
और ख़ारिशज़दा[9] से कुछ कुत्ते
लेटे रहते हैं बे-नियाज़ाना[10]
दुम मरोड़े कि कोई सर कुचले
काटना क्या, वो भौंकते भी नहीं

और जब वो दहकता अंगारा
छन से सागर में डूब जाता है
तीरगी[11] ओढ़ लेती है दुनिया
कश्तियाँ कुछ किनारे आती हैं
भंग, गांजा, चरस, शराब, अफ़्यून
जो भी लायें, जहाँ से भी लायें
दौड़ते हैं इधर से कुछ साये
और सब कुछ उतार लाते हैं

गाड़ी जाती है अद्ल[12] की मीज़ान[13]
जिसका हिस्सा उसी को मिलता है
यहाँ ख़तरा नहीं ख़यानत[14] का
तुम यहाँ क्यों खड़े हो मुद्दत से
ये तुम्हारी थकी-थकी भेड़ें
रात जिनकों ज़मीं के सीने पर
सुब्ह होते उंडेल देती है
मंडियों, दफ़्तरों, मिलों की तरफ़

---

9. खुजली रोग से पीड़ित, 10. निश्चिंत 11. अंधेरा, 12. न्याय, 13. तराज़ू.
14. बेईमानी, विश्वासघात।

The huts are encircled by a desolation
Where fish dry during the day
Cats sit watching from afar
And scabies-ridden dogs
Lie around without a care
Far from biting, they don't even bark.

When that smouldering ember
Sinks suddenly into the ocean
The world covers itself with darkness,
Some boats come ashore
With bhang, hashish, smack, alcohol, opium
Whatever they bring, from wherever they bring
Some shadows run from here
And unload everything on the shore.

The scales of justice are buried
Each one receives what he deserves,
There's no danger here of betrayal
Why have you been standing here since ages?
Here are your tired sheep
That, from the earth's depths, the night
Throws out everyday at dawn
Towards markets, offices and mills

हाँक देती, ढकेल देती है
रास्ते में ये रुक नहीं सकतीं
तोड़ के घुटने झुक नहीं सकतीं
इनसे तुम क्या तव्वक़ो[15] रखते हो
भेड़िया इनके साथ चलता है

तकते रहते हो उस सड़क की तरफ़
दफ़्न जिसमें कई कहानियाँ हैं
दफ़्न जिसमें कई जवानियाँ हैं
जिस पे इक साथ भागी फिरती हैं
ख़ाली जेबें भी और तिजोरियाँ भी
जाने किसका है इंतिज़ार तुम्हें

मुझको देखो कि मैं वही तो हूँ
जिसको कोड़ों की छाँव में दुनिया
बेचती भी ख़रीदती भी थी

मुझको देखो कि मैं वही तो हूँ
जिसको खेतों से ऐसा बाँधा था
जैसे मैं उनका एक हिस्सा था
खेत बिकते तो मैं भी बिकता था

मुझको देखो कि मैं वही तो हूँ
कुछ मशीनें बनायीं जब मैंने
उन मशीनों के मालिकों ने मुझे
बे-झिझक उनमें ऐसे झोंक दिया
जैसे मैं कुछ नहीं हूँ ईंधन हूँ

---

15. अपेक्षा।

Pushing and prodding them along
They cannot stop on the way
Cannot flex their knees to bend
What do you expect from them after all?
The wolf with them walks along.

You keep looking towards the road
Where many tales lie buried
Where the youth of many is buried
Where travel together
Both empty pockets and treasuries
I wonder which one you are waiting for.

Look at me, for I am he
Who in the shadows of whips
The world used to buy and sell.

Look at me, for I am he
Who was tied to the fields
As though a part of them,
When the fields were sold I was sold with them.

Look at me, for I am he
Who made a few machines and
By their owners
Was dumped into them unhesitatingly
As though I were mere fuel.

मुझको देखो कि मैं थका-हारा
फिर रहा हूँ युगों से आवारा
तुम यहाँ से हटो तो आज की रात
सो रहूँ मैं इसी चबूतरे पर
तुम यहाँ से हटो खुदा के लिए

जाओ, वो वियतनाम के जंगल
उसके मसलूब[16] शहर, ज़ख्मी गाँव
जिनको इंजील[17] पढ़ने वालों ने
रौंद डाला है फूँक डाला है
जाने कब से पुकारते हैं तुम्हें

जाओ, इक बार फिर हमारे लिए
तुमको चढ़ना पड़ेगा सूली पर

---

16. सलीब (सूली) पर चढ़ाये गये, 17. बाइबिल।

Look at me who, tired and defeated,
Has been roving like a vagabond for years,
If you move from here, then tonight
I will sleep on this veranda
For God's sake move from here.

Go to the jungles of Vietnam
Its crucified cities and wounded villages
Which have by the Bible readers
Been crushed and burnt,
Go, they have been calling out to you for ages.

Go, once more for our sake,
You will have to ascend the stake.

दूसरा तूफ़ान

और फिर एक रात ऐसी आयी
मयकदे[1] बुझ गये
सारे आतिशकदे[2] बुझ गये
मयकदों और आतिशकदों के रक़ीब[3]
इक मुजाहिद[4] अदीब[5]
ज़िंदगी के लिए
जो हमेशा मशीयत[6] से लड़ता रहा
आदमी के लिए
जो ख़ुदा का गरेबाँ पकड़ता रहा
लड़ते-लड़ते वो इक रोज़ चुप हो गया
अपने ही इक सहीफ़े[7] से मुँह ढाँप के सो गया
लेकिन उसका क़लम
जिसके सौ नाम हैं
जिसके सौ काम हैं
लड़ रहा है उसी ढंग से आज तक
चल रहा है उसी रंग से आज तक
गाह[8] इस हाथ में
गाह उस हाथ में
चलते-चलते कई उँगलियाँ मुड़ गयीं
और कई उँगलियों ने बुनीं
नित नयी साज़िशें
नित नयी रस्सियाँ

---

1. मदिरालय. 2. पारसियों का उपासना गृह. 3. प्रतिद्वन्दी 4. संघर्ष (जिहाद) करने
वाला. 5. साहित्यकार. 6. देवशक्ति, ईश्वर की इच्छा. 7. पुस्तक. 8. कभी

Second Storm

And then came a night
When bars shut down
All fire temples shut down.
He, who opposed the bars and temples,
A writer, willing to fight
For life,
Who had always fought against the will of God,
For man
Had been willing to take on even God
One day, while fighting, fell silent,
Covering his face with one of his books slept.
But his pen,
Which has a hundred names
And does a hundred things,
Is fighting in the same way still
It moves on in the same pace
Sometimes in this hand
Sometimes in another
Moving on, some fingers bent,
While others busy spinning
New conspiracies everyday
New ropes everyday

और फिर उसको सूली पर लटका दिया
अर्श[9] से कोई पैग़ाम आया नहीं
आसमानों पे उसको बुलाया नहीं
उसकी टूटी हुई पसलियों से मगर
इस तरह ख़ून रिसने-टपकने लगा
रस्सियाँ जल गयीं
साज़िशें गल गयीं
नूह[10] के अहद[11] का ये फ़साना नहीं
आज की बात है
उसने नोके-ज़बाँ[12] पर समंदर उठाया
उठाकर फ़िज़ाओं में फैला दिया
कुर-ए-अर्ज़[13] को ले के मिनक़ार[14] में
यूँ उछाला ख़लाओं[15] में लटका दिया
दश्तो-दर[16] काँप उठे
बहरो-बर[17] काँप उठे
बे-ख़बर काँप उठे
बा-ख़बर काँप उठे
ये वो तूफ़ाँ नहीं डूब जाती है जिसमें ज़मीं
इसमें डूबी ज़मीनें उभर आती हैं

---

9. आकाश, 10. पैग़म्बर नूह, जिनके समय में प्रलयंकर तूफ़ान आया था और जिन्होंने अपनी किश्ती में हर जाति के प्राणी का एक-एक जोड़ा बचा लिया था जिससे प्राणी जगत् का क्रम चलता रहा, 11. युग, 12. जिह्वा की नोक, 13. भूमंडल, 14 चोंच, 15. शून्य, 16. जंगल और बस्ती, 17. जल-थल।

Hanged him from a stake.
No messages came from the skies
The heavens did not call him up,
But from his broken bones
The blood flowed in such a way
The ropes burnt
The conspiracies rotted away.
This is not a tale from Noah's time
It is a story of today,
He held the ocean on the tip of his tongue
And swung it into the sphere,
Picked up the earth in his beak
And tossed it in to the void.
Forests and towns trembled
The ignorant trembled
The learned trembled.
This is not the storm in which the earth drowns
In this storm, the drowned earth emerges again.

रक्क़ास[1] शरारा[2]

दो निगाहों का अचानक वह तसादुम,[3] तोबा
ठेस लगते ही उड़ा इश्क़ शरारा बनकर

उड़के पहले उन्हीं झेंपी हुई नज़रों में रुका
नर्म, मासूम, हसीं, मस्त इशारा बनकर

फिर निगह से अर्क़-आलूद[4] जबीं[5] पर झलका
पंखड़ी, फूल, गुहर[6] लाल, सितारा बनकर

ढलके माथे से उतर आया गुले-आरिज़[7] में
रंग, रस, शहद, नहीं इनसे भी प्यारा बनकर

गुले-आरिज़ से सिमट आया लबे-रंगीं में
राग, मय, लहर, हँसी, बर्क़[8] का धारा बनकर

लबे-गुलरंग से फिर रेंग गया बाँहों में
लोच, ख़म, जज़्ब[9] मचलता हुआ पारा बनकर

बसके बाँहों की गुदाज़ी[10] मैं चला दिल की तरफ़
चाह, अल्ताफ़[11] करम, प्यार, मुदारा[12] बनकर

दिल में डूबा था कि बस फूट पड़ा रग-रग से
जाने-दिल, जाने-नज़र, जाने नज़ारा बनकर

---

1. नाचती हुई. 2. चिनगारी. 3. टकराव. 4. भीगा हुआ. 5. माथा. 6. मोती. 7. गालों के फूल. 8. बिजली. 9. आकर्षण. 10. मांसलता. 11. कृपा. 12. सत्कार, आवभगत।

A Dancing Spark

Suddenly two glances collided with such impact,
That love was like a spark set adrift in time.

First it rested in those bashful eyes
Like a tender, innocent, lovely, drunken sign,

Then it fluttered to her glistening forehead
Like a bud, a flower, a pearl, a star pristine.

From her forehead it descended to her petalled cheeks
As colour, essence, honey, no even more divine.

Down her cheeks it withdrew into the colour of her lips
As music, wine, laughter, the lightning's outline.

From her lips it slithered into her arms
As a curve, an enticement, mercury's dancing line.

Interred in her arms, it went towards the heart.
As desire, grace, favour, love, courtsey benign

Once drowned in the heart, it broke from every pore
As the heart's beat, the gaze's soul, the horizon's shine.

पैकरे-हुस्न[13] से फिर उड़ के चला मेरी तरफ़
एक बदमस्त जवानी का उतारा बनकर

रहज़ने-होश[14] मगर होश का पैग़ाम लिये
दुश्मने-ज़ब्त[15] मगर ज़ब्त का यारा[16] बनकर

दर्द ही दर्द मगर वज़्हे-सुकूँ[17] वज़्हे-तरब[18]
सोज़ ही सोज़ मगर जान से प्यार बनकर

आते ही छा गया खोयी हुई हस्ती पे मेरी
मेरी खोयी हुई हस्ती का सहारा बनकर

अब शरारा यही उसके दिले-बेदार में है
और 'कैफ़ी' मेरे तपते हुए अशआर[19] में है

---

13. रूप की काया, 14. चेतना का बटमार, 15. धीरज का शत्रू, 16. संबल, अबलंब.
17. शांति का कारण, 18. उल्लास का कारण, 19. कविता (शेर का बहुवचन)।

From the body's charm, it flew towards me
Like a drunken youthfulness' irresistible anodyne.

Stealing senses, yet carrying a sensible message
Strengthening restraint, even if destroying its design.

Pain incarnate, yet the reason for joy
Passion itself, yet a part of love sublime.

The moment it came it encompassed my life
By becoming my lost life's supporting line.

Now sparks alone rest in her heart
And 'Kaifi', my burning couplets define.

एहतियात

अब तुम आग़ोशे-तसव्वुर¹ में भी आया न करो
मुझसे बिखरे हुए गेसू² नहीं देखे जाते
सुर्ख़ आँखों की क़सम, काँपती पलकों की क़सम
थरथराते हुए आँसू नहीं देखे जाते

अब तुम आग़ोशे-तसव्वुर में भी आया न करो
छूट जाने दो जो दामने-वफ़ा छूट गया
क्यूँ ये नाज़ीदा-ख़िरामी³ पे पशीमाँ-नज़री⁴
तुमने तोड़ा तो नहीं रिश्तए-दिल टूट गया

अब तुम आग़ोशे-तसव्वुर में भी आया न करो
मेरी आहों से ये रुख़सार⁵ न कुम्हला जायें
ढूँढती होगी तुम्हें रस में नहायी हुई रात
जाओ कलियाँ न कहीं सेज की मुरझा जायें

अब तुम आग़ोशे-तसव्वुर में भी आया न करो
मैं इस उजड़े हुए पहलू में बिठा लूं न कहीं
लबे-शीरीं⁶ का नमक, आरिज़े-नमकीं⁷ की मिठास
अपने तरसे हुए होंटों से चुरा लूँ न कहीं

अब तुम आग़ोशे-तसव्वुर में भी आया न करो
तुमको ये रस्म भी दुनिया न निभाने देगी
बढ़के दामन से लिपट जायेगी यूँ ताज़ा बहार
मेरी आग़ोशे-तसव्वुर में न आने देगी

---

1. कल्पना की गोद (परिधि), 2. बाल, 3. नाज से चलना, 4. लज्जित होकर देखना,
5. गाल, 6. मीठे होंठ, 7. नमकीन गाल।

Caution

Do not come to me now even in my thoughts
Your tangled tresses I cannot bear to see,
By the redness of my eyes, by my trembling lashes, I swear
Your copious tears, I cannot bear to see.

Do not come to me now even in my thoughts
If the bond of fidelity is broken, let it go,
What need of shame to gaze at your seductive walk
You didn't break it but this pledge with the heart is gone.

Do not come to me now even in my thoughts
The glow on your cheeks may be dimmed by my sigh,
The night, bathed in joy, must be searching for you
Go before the buds in your flowerbed die.

Do not come to me now even in my thoughts
Lest in a desolate corner I keep you tucked away,
The sweetness of your lips, the tang of your cheeks
What if my thirsty lips steal them away.

Do not come to me now even in my thoughts
The world will not allow you to fulfil this task,
The spring, just arrived, will take you in its arms
And prevent you from being in my thought's clasp.

औरत

उठ मेरी जान! मेरे साथ ही चलना है तुझे

कल्बे-माहौल[1] में लरज़ाँ[2] शररे-जंग[3] हैं आज
हौसले वक़्त के और ज़ीस्त[4] के यकरंग हैं आज
आबगीनों[5] में तपाँ वलवलए-संग[6] हैं आज
हुस्न और इश्क़ हम आवाज़ो-हमआहंग[7] हैं आज
जिस में जलता हूँ उसी आग में जलना है तुझे

उठ मेरी जान! मेरे साथ ही चलना है तुझे

ज़िंदगी जेहद[10] में है सब्र के क़ाबू में नहीं
नब्ज़े-हस्ती का लहू काँपती आँसू में नहीं
उड़ने खुलने में है नकहत[11] ख़मे-गेसू[12] में नहीं
जन्नत इक और है जो मर्द के पहलू में नहीं
उसकी आज़ाद रविश पर भी मचलना है तुझे

उठ मेरी जान! मेरे साथ ही चलना है तुझे

गोशे-गोशे[13] में सुलगती है चिता तेरे लिए
फ़र्ज़ का भेस बदलती है क़ज़ा[14] तेरे लिए
क़हर[15] है तेरी हर इक नर्म अदा तेरे लिए
ज़हर ही ज़हर है दुनिया की हवा तेरे लिए
रुत बदल डाल अगर फूलना-फलना है तुझे

उठ मेरी जान! मेरे साथ ही चलना है तुझे

क़द्र अब तक तेरी तारीख़[16] ने जानी ही नहीं

---

1. वातावरण का मर्मस्थल (हृदय), 2. कंपित, 3. युद्ध की चिंगारियाँ, 4. जीवन,
5. शराब की बोतल, 6. पत्थर की उमंग, 7. एक स्वर और एक लय रखने वाले,
8. पारा, 9. पात्र, 10. संघर्ष, 11. महक, 12. बालों के घुमाव (घूंघर) 13. कोने-कोने,
14. मृत्यु, 15. प्रलय, विनाश, 16. इतिहास,

Woman

Rise, my love! You have to walk along with me

Sparks of rebellion are astir in the air, today
Both time and life have but one resolve, today
Rocks swirl around in delicate decanters, today
Love and beauty have one voice, today.
In the fire I burn you too must burn with me

Rise my love! You have to walk along with me.

Life lies in battle, not in patience and restraint only
Life's veins have blood, not trembling tears only
In what opens and flies lies fragrance, not in tresses only
There is a paradise too, beyond a male's embrace only.
To its free rhythm you have to dance in ecstasy

Rise my love! You have to walk along with me.

In every corner a pyre smoulders for you
Death changes the garb of duty for you
Elegance is an invitation to destruction for you
The world is nothing but poison for you.
Change the season if you want to blossom too

Rise my love! You have to walk along with me.

History has not yet known to respect you

तुझमें शोले भी है बस अश्क़फ़िशानी[17] ही नहीं
तू हक़ीक़त भी है दिलचस्प कहानी ही नहीं
तेरी हस्ती भी है इक चीज़ जवानी ही नहीं
अपनी तारीख़ का उनवान[18] बदलना है तुझे

उठ मेरी जान! मेरे साथ ही चलना है तुझे

तोड़कर रस्म के बुत बंदे-क़दामत[19] से निकल
ज़ोफ़े-इशरत[20] से निकल, वहमे-नज़ाकत[21] से निकल
नफ़्स[22] के खींचे हुए हल्क़े-ए-अज़मत[23] से निकल
यह भी इक क़ैद ही है, क़ैदे-मुहब्बत से निकल
राह का ख़ार ही क्या गुल भी कुचलना है तुझे

उठ मेरी जान! मेरे साथ ही चलना है तुझे

तोड़ यह अज़्म-शिकन[24] दग़दग़ए-पंद[25] भी तोड़
तेरी ख़ातिर है जो ज़ंजीर वह सौगंध भी तोड़
तौक़ यह भी ज़म्मरुद का गुलूबंद भी तोड़
तोड़ पैमानए-मर्दाने-ख़िरदमंद[26] भी तोड़
बनके तूफ़ान छलकना है उबलना है तुझे

उठ मेरी जान! मेरे साथ ही चलना है तुझे

तू फ़लातूनो-अरस्तू है तू जुहरा[27] परवीं[28]
तेरे क़ब्ज़े में है गर्दूं[29], तेरी ठोकर में ज़मीं
हाँ, उठा, जल्द उठा पाए-मुक़क़दर[30] से जबीं[31]
मैं भी रुकने का नहीं, वक़्त भी रुकने का नहीं
लड़खड़ायेगी कहाँ तक कि सँभलना है तुझे

उठ मेरी जान! मेरे साथ ही चलना है तुझे

---

17. आँसू बहाना, 18. शीर्षक, 19. प्राचीनता के बंधन, 20. ऐश्वर्य की दुर्बलता, 21. कोमलता का भ्रम, 22. आकांक्षा, कामना, 23 महानता का वृत, 24. संकल्प भंग करने वाला, 25. उपदेश की आशंका, 26. समझदार पुरुषों के मापदंडए, 27. शुक्र ग्रह, 28. कृत्तिका नक्षत्र (सुंदरता का प्रतीक), 29. आकाश, 30. भाग्य के चरण, 31. माथा।

Not only tears, there are glowing embers within you
Not entertaining stories only, there is a reality to you
Not only your youth, your existence has value too.
You have to change the title of your history

Rise my love! You have to walk along with me.

Break the bond of custom, from the prison of tradition escape
Delight not in your weakness, from this imagined delicacy
                                                escape
From these self-conjured vows of greatness escape
It too is bondage, from love's bondage escape.
Not only the thorn, the flower too emasculate

Rise my love! You have to walk along with me.

Break these doubts, the uncertainties about what is right, break
The vow that for you is a fetter, break
It is a yoke of emeralds, even this necklace break
Break the standards set by so-called wise men, break!
Becoming a storm, you have to walk along with me

Rise my love! You have to walk along with me.

You are Aristotle's philosophy, you are the symbol of beauty
The sky is in your palm, foreheads at your feet
Yes, raise, raise quickly your forehead from the feet of destiny
I too will not tarry, nor will time wait for any.
How long will you falter, you must have stability

Rise my love! You have to walk along with me.

एक बोसा

जब भी चूम लेता हूँ इन हसीन आँखों को
सौ चिराग़ अँधेरे में झिलमिलाने लगते हैं

फूल क्या, शिगूफ़े' क्या, चाँद क्या, सितारे क्या,
सब रक़ीब² क़दमों पर सर झुकाने लगते हैं

रक़्स³ करने लगती हैं मूरतें अजंता की
मुद्दतों के लबबस्ता⁴ ग़ार⁵ गाने लगते हैं

फूल खिलने लगते हैं उजड़े-उजड़े गुलशन⁶ में
प्यासी-प्यासी धरती पर अब्र⁷ छाने लगते हैं

लम्हे भर को ये दुनिया जुल्म छोड़ देती है
लम्हे भर को सब पत्थर मुस्कराने लगते हैं

---

1. कलियाँ, 2. प्रतिद्वन्द्वी, 3. नृत्य, 4. जिनके होंट बंद हों, 5. गुफाएँ, 6. उपवन,
7. बादल।

A Kiss

Whenever I kiss these beautiful eyes
A hundred candles begin to glow in the dark.

Not only flowers, or buds, or the moon, or stars
At her feet even the rival bows.

The statues of Ajanta begin to dance
Caves long silent burst into song.

Gardens long neglected begin to bloom
Rain clouds start gathering on a thirsty earth.

For a moment this world renounces crime
For a moment even stones begin to smile.

ज़िंदगी

आज अँधेरा मेरी नस-नस में उतर जायेगा
आँखें बुझ जायेंगी, बुझ जायेंगे एहसासो-शऊर[1]
और यह सदियों से जलता-सा सुलगता-सा वजूद[2]
इससे पहले कि सहर[3] माथे पे शबनम[4] छिड़के
इससे पहले कि मेरी बेटी के वह फूल से हाथ
गर्म रुख़सार[5] को ठंडक बख्शें
इससे पहले कि मेरे बेटे का मज़बूत बदन
तने मफ़लूज[6] में शक्ति भर दे
इससे पहले कि मेरे बीवी के होंट
मेरे होंटों की तपिश पी जायें
राख हो जायेगा जलते-जलते
और फिर राख बिखर जायेगी
ज़िंदगी कहने को बे-माया[7] सही
ग़म का सरमाया[8] सही
मैंने इसके लिए क्या-क्या न किया
कभी आसानी से इक साँस भी यमराज को अपना न दिया

आज से पहले बहुत पहले
इसी आँगन में
धूप भरे दामन में
मैं खड़ा था, मेरे तलवों से धुआँ उठता था

---

1. अनुभूति तथा चेतना. 2. अस्तित्व. 3. प्रभात. 4. ओस. 5. गाल. 6. अपंग शरीर.
7. जिसके पास कुछ न हो. अकिंचन, 8. पूँजी।

Life

Today, the darkness will descend in all my pores
Eyes will close, feeling and consciousness will die
And this reality, smouldering since centuries, will be no more.
Before the dawn sprinkles dew on my forehead,
Before the flowerlike hands of my daughter
Cool my fevered cheeks,
Before the strong body of my son
Fills this disabled body with strength,
Before the lips of my wife
Drink the thirst of my lips,
Everything will turn to ashes
And then this ash will disperse.
Perhaps it is true that life has nothing
Maybe its only treasure is sorrow
Yet, what have I not done for it?
Not a single breath have I readily given Yamraj.

Long ago, much before today
In this very courtyard
In this sun-dappled home
I stood, and smoke rose from my soles

एक बेनाम सा बेरंग सा ख़ौफ़
कच्चे एहसास पे छाया था कि जल जाऊँगा
मैं पिघल जाऊँगा
और पिघलकर मेरा कमज़ोर-सा 'मैं'
क़तरा-क़तरा मेरे माथे से टपक जायेगा
रो रहा था मगर अश्कों के बगैर
चीख़ता था मगर आवाज़ न थी
मौत लहराती थी सौ शक्लों में
मैंने हर शक्ल को घबरा के ख़ुदा मान लिया
काट के रख दिये संदल के पुरअसरार[9] दरख़्त[10]
और पत्थर से निकाला शोला
और रौशन किया अपने से बड़ा एक अलाव
जानवर ज़िब्ह[11] किये इतने कि ख़ूँ की लहरें
पाँव से उठके कमर तक आयीं
और कमर से मेरे सर तक आयीं

सोमरस मैंने पिया
रात-दिन रक़्स[12] किया
नाचते-नाचते तलवे मेरे ख़ूँ देने लगे
मेरे आज़ा[13] की थकन
बन गयी काँपते होंटों पे भजन
हड्डियाँ मेरी चटख़ने लगीं ईंधन की तरह
मंत्र होंटों से टपकने लगे रौग़न[14] की तरह
'अग्नि माता मेरी अग्नि माता
सूखी लकड़ी के ये भारी कुंदे

---

9. रहस्यमय, 10. पेड़, 11. पशु बलि, 12. नृत्य, 13. अंग (अज्व बहुवचन),
14. तेल, चिकनाई।

An unnamed, formless fear
That I would burn, spread over my fragile emotions
That I would melt
And having melted, my weak sense of 'I'
Would drip, drop by drop, from my forehead.
I cried, but there were no tears
I screamed, but there was no sound.
Death hovered around with a hundred faces
In despair, I accepted each face as God,
I cut aside mysterious sandalwood trees
From stone I scooped burning embers
And illumined a space larger than myself
Sacrificed so many animals that rivers of blood
Rose from my feet to my waist
And from my waist to my head.

I drank *somras*
Danced night and day
Until blood flowed from my soles
The fatigue of my body
Became, on trembling lips, a prayer,
My bones groaned like wood on fire
Mantras slipped smoothly from my lips
'O fire-goddess, my fire-mother
These heavy earrings of dry wood

जो तेरी भेंट को ले आया हूँ
उनको स्वीकार कर और ऐसे धधक
कि मचलते शोले
खींच लें जोश में
सूरज की सुनहरी जुल्फें
आग में आग मिले;
जो अमर कर दे मुझे
ऐसा कोई राग मिले।'

अग्नि माँ से भी न जीने की सनद जब पायी
ज़िंदगी के नये इमकान[15] ने ली अँगड़ाई
और कानों में कहीं दूर से आवाज़ आयी
बुद्धं शरणं गच्छामि!
धम्मं शरणं गच्छामि!
संघं शरणं गच्छामि!

चार अबरू[16] का सफ़ाया करके
बेसिले वस्त्र से ढाँपा यह बदन
पोंछ के पत्नी के माथे से दमकती.बिंदिया
सोते बच्चों को बिना प्यार किये
चल पड़ा हाथ में कशकोल[17] लिये
चाहता था कहीं भिक्षा ही में जीवन मिल जाये,
जो कभी बंद न हो, दिल को वह धड़कन मिल जाये
मुझको भिक्षा में मगर ज़हर मिला
होंठ थर्राने लगे जैसे करे कोई गिला[18]
झुक के सूली से उसी वक़्त किसी ने यह कहा
तेरे इक गाल पे जिस पल कोई थप्पड़ मारे
दूसरा गाल भी आगे कर दे

---

15. संभावना, 16. भौं जो आँखों के ऊपर होती है, 17. भिक्षा-पात्र, 18. शिकायत।

That I have brought for you as a gift
Please accept them and burn so fiercely
That your dancing embers
Draw in joyously
The sun's golden locks
Let fire meet with fire;
One which makes me immortal
That *raaga* I hope to find one day.'
When fire-mother too did not grant the benediction of life
A new possibility of life came alive
And from a distance came the voice:
Budham Sharnam Gachchami!
Dhammam Sharnam Gachchami!
Sangham Sharnam Gachchami!
I shaved my head clean
Clad myself in unstitched clothes,
Wiping away the glowing *bindiya* from my wife's forehead
Without caressing my sleeping children
I left with a begging bowl in my hands
I wished to find a life in alms
And a heartbeat that would never stop.
But I was given poison in alms,
As if making a complaint, my lips shuddered
Just then, someone bent down from the gallows to say:
If somcone slaps one of your cheeks
Offer him the other one too

तेरी दुनिया में बहुत हिंसा है
इसके सीने में अहिंसा भर दे
कि यह जीने का तरीक़ा भी है अंदाज़ भी है
तेरी आवाज़ भी है, मेरी आवाज़ भी है
मैं उठा जिसको अहिंसा का सबक़ सिखलाने
मुझको लटका दिया सूली पे उसी दुनिया ने
आ रहा था मैं कई कूचों से ठोकर खाकर
एक आवाज़ ने रोका मुझको
किसी मीनार से नीचे आकर
अल्लाहो अकबर[19] अल्लाहो अकबर
हुआ दिल को यह गुमाँ[20]
कि यह पुरजोश अज़ाँ[21]
मौत से देगी अमाँ[22]
फिर तो पहुँचा मैं जहाँ
मैंने दोहरायी कुछ ऐसे यह अज़ाँ
गूँज उठा सारा जहाँ
अल्लाहो अकबर, अल्लाहो अकबर
उसी आवाज़ में इक और भो गूँजा ऐलान
कुल्ले मिन अलेहा फ़ान[23]
इक तरफ़ ढल गया ख़ुरशीदे-जहाँताब[24] का सर
हुआ फ़ालिज का असर
फट गयी नस कोई, शिरयानों[25] में ख़ूँ जम सा गया
हो गया ज़ख़्मी दिमाग़
ऐसा लगता था कि बुझ जायेगा जलता है जो सदियों से चिराग़
आज अँधेरा मेरी नस-नस में उतर जायेगा

---

19. ईश्वर महान है, 20. भ्रम, 21. नमाज़ का 22. सुरक्षा, 23. हर वस्तु नश्वर है,
24. सारे संसार को आलोकित करने वाला सूर्य, 25. धमनियों।

There is too much violence in your world
Fill your heart with non-violence
That too is a way of life
There is your voice, and mine too.
But alas, the ones I set out to teach non-violence to
Were the ones who hung me from the stake.
As I returned rejected from many paths
A voice stopped me in my tracks
It wafted down from the tower
Allah-O-Akbar, Allah-O-Akbar
The heart was deluded to believe
That this resounding call of the *azaan*
Would protect me from death
Of course, I went there.
I repeated that call in such a way
That the whole world resounded with it
Allah-O Akbar, Allah-O Akbar.
In that call was one more voice,
Everything must perish
Even the sun, life-giver to all, must set.
A paralysis overtook me
A vein burst, the blood congealed in the arteries,
The mind was wounded
It seemed as if the lamp, for centuries alight, would die
A darkness would descend in all my pores.

यह समंदर जो बड़ी देर से तूफ़ानी था
ऐसा तड़पा कि मेरे कमरे के अंदर आया
आते-आते वह मेरे वास्ते अमृत लाया
और लहरा के कहा
शिव ने यह भिजवाया है, लो पियो और जियो
आज शिव इल्म है, अमृत है अमल
अब वह आसाँ है दुश्वार था कल
रात जो मौत का पैग़ाम लिये आयी थी
बीवी-बच्चों ने मेरे
उसको खिड़की से परे फेंक दिया
और जो वह ज़हर का इक जाम लिये आयी थी
उसने वह ख़ुद ही पिया
सुब्ह उतरी जो समंदर में नहाने के लिए
रात की लाश मिली पानी में

This ocean, stormy for so long
Took such a turn that it entered my room,
It came with *amrit* for me
And, rising and falling, it said,
Shiva has sent this, drink it and live
Today, Shiva is knowledge, *amrit* is truth.
Now, what was difficult yesterday has become easy.
The message of death that the night had brought
Was flung out of the window
By my wife and children.
And the poison it had come with
It sipped itself,
In the morning when it entered the ocean to bathe
Its corpse was found in the water's waste.